HERE LIES THE TRUTH

Kionna Bass

HERE LIES THE TRUTH

KIONNA BASS

ISBN: 978-1-951838-24-9

Portions of this book are works of nonfiction.

Published By: 90 Day Legacy Builders

SouthPaw Writing & Editing
Jocelyn "Vee" McElroy
southpaw.wred@gmail.com
404-590-1506

TABLE OF CONTENTS

Introduction i

Foreword ii

Chapter 1: In the Beginning 1

Chapter 2: High School 7

Chapter 3: Better Days 13

Chapter 4: Three's A Crowd 17

Chapter 5: The Firsts 23

Chapter 6: Summer 2011 32

Chapter 7: Only the Beginning 38

Chapter 8: 2013 49

Chapter 9: A Turnaround 66

Chapter 10: Life Post-College 75

Chapter 11: 2015 81

Chapter 12: A Whole New World 101

Chapter 13: Chapter 24 108

Chapter 14: Birth of A Savage 132

Chapter 15: Lost 142

Chapter 16: Found 156

Chapter 17: More Life 160

INTRODUCTION

This book is to inform you that my life has not been perfect, but God has been. Even through my disobedience, God still covered me and loved me despite my ways. What if the one thing you thought was sent to break you was the very thing that made you? What if it gave you a new strength and a new purpose? Life is not a race, it's a walk. It's about learning from mistakes and walking in wisdom. God is so amazing that even through sin and disobedience He still blesses us. I am, and forever will be, thankful that He is gracious enough to get us out of the mess that we caused ourselves.

This is not a feel-good book; so, if you're looking for that, put this book down. If you're holier than thou, put it down. This book is raw; it's uncut. It's me. It's my story. It's my walk. Here lies the truth.

FOREWORD

Knowing a person starts with understanding their truth. In that process you build a foundation. When creating a foundation, you must dig deep and then deeper into their dirt. Dirt brings so many things to flourish like life, flowers, and food, but it can also bring death and destruction. When you read this story, you will see how a young vulnerable princess transforms into a beautiful and educated Black Queen. As a teenager, her words had always been powerful and influential. As a woman, her words are encouraging and motivating. So, here lies the truth.

Love you,

-Delaine

CHAPTER ONE

IN THE BEGINNING

There were five of us. Pops, Mama, my older sister Toria, little brother Kasen, and me. Then there were four—after the divorce, of course. My sister and I are only two years apart. We were old enough to start noticing things like more yelling, more tears, and more fights. Things weren't the same in our household. The love had grown cold...or what I thought was love anyway. We went to our grandparents' house in Louisiana like we always did for the summer. But when we came back, things had changed. We didn't go back to our big three-bedroom house with the bonus room full of toys and a playground for a backyard. Instead, mommy took us to an apartment. I'll never forget the smell of fresh paint and the empty feeling in a space full of clutter. I remember things not being fully unpacked and looking around confused.

Mommy said, "This is going to be our new home for a little while." So, naturally, we had questions as all little kids do. I specifically remember the question "Where is Daddy, and when is he coming home?" I'm sure she knew it was coming. Surely, she dreaded this question and thought about it all summer while we were away. With the world's fakest smile, she choked up the words "He's not coming. Your dad and I are getting a divorce."

Tears and confusion filled the room. How could she explain to adolescent children the severity of a broken marriage? Why should she have to? Was it even our business? Would we have even comprehended? Questions filled my mind. What happened? Why do we have to live here? What about school? Will you guys get back together? I was only 6, maybe 7. I didn't know exactly what a divorce was, but I knew it meant they didn't love each other anymore. I knew that life as I knew it was over. What I didn't know was that this was the beginning of heartbreak—not only for my parents but for us as well. While I won't share my siblings' inner struggles—as I do not know them as my own—I do know that I found out what heartbreak was at age 7.

Life goes on...

Life was definitely a little—well...very different. School was the same, mostly. I can't remember how my teachers found out about my parents' "die-vorce", as I like to call it, but knowing me it probably was my big mouth. I was in the second grade, and we had gotten a take home assignment. I remember my teacher asked me at whose house I was going to be for the time being. Embarrassed, I answered, "I don't know", as I couldn't keep up with the custody agreements. It was too much for a 7-year-old to keep track of.

I can remember Daddy being the "cool" parent. We could stay up later at his house, listen to secular music, watch the good tv shows—all that jazz. But that was a short-lived fantasy. One day Daddy picked us up from Mommy and brought us to the house I knew to be "home". We walked in and he introduced this lady. Honestly, I can't remember who he introduced her to be, but I knew she was more than a friend. I knew she had taken over my mother's throne. I've always been mature for my age, so I knew something was up...I just had not put my finger on it. Needless to say, she'd gotten the side-eye.

As time went on, they became more public with their relationship and started spending more time together. Seemed like I hardly ever spent any alone time with my dad because she was always there. I didn't mind that much because I was young and incapable of understanding what was about to transpire.

Now, finally settled into the rotation between Mommy's house and Daddy's house, lesson number one was learned: *never get used to anything.* Ok guys, time travel with me back to the summer of 2000. Setting: Grandma's house. Daddy calls to talk to us on the phone. We're doing the typical "I miss you too", "Yes I've been good"," Yes it's hot", and "No I'm not ready to come home and start school" song and dance.

Daddy: I have something to tell you. I'm moving to Atlanta.

Tickled pink, I laughed.

3

Him: I'm serious.

At this point, I got quiet. I was trying to choke down that lump of sadness, tears, fear, etc. It was my first of many shots of fireball. Oh, how it burned like fire. I remember fighting back the tears and asking "Why?" I was a "why" kid. He told me he found a job there and it would be good for him. I automatically went into question mode. "When will I see you?" "How often?" "Don't you think that's too far?" Panic mode. I felt like my dad was going to the store to get milk and never returning. Lesson number two: *never panic.* The custody agreement must have changed. Of course, we saw him less. But when we did spend time together, I clung to his every teaching and every word.

I occupied my years of adolescence with school, friends, writing music, poetry, and softball. Softball was something I loved. It was a stress reliever. Expensive and hard on a pocketbook—but Mama enjoyed watching me play. She was definitely my number one fan. I can hear her now yelling at the umpire, "BLUE, BLUE, DON'T YOU STRIKE MY BABY OUT!!" She boosted me like I was an all-star or some-thing, but I was just "aight". She did not miss many games. She'd be out there with her ballpark chair and her peanuts talking trash and joking around with the other parents. Yes, plural. Parents. Salt alert.

It was typical to be the only black girl on the team. It was something I was used to. The older I got, the better I became. I started playing softball for the Amateur Athletic Union...even more of a pocketbook robber. Mommy felt like I was worth it, so she did what she had to do to afford me the opportunity to be great. There weren't many single parents out there with my mom. There were a lot of dads out there though, teaching and coaching their daughters. Then there was me, hanging on to the hope that maybe Daddy will come to this game today.

Anyone who knows me knows that I tend to always give people the benefit of the doubt. So, Daddy was busy, or working, or whatever other excuse I had formulated in my mind. I remember needing new equipment—bats, gloves, cleats, etc. Playing from February to November, bats did not last long...maybe two seasons if you're careful and lucky. Mommy would always set me up for the okey-doke saying, "Go ask your dad". So being a child, I asked. His excuses varied between "I don't have any money right now" or "Ask your mom, I send child support." I heard this from the time I was eight through my senior year of high school. For a while I believed, between the second and third ring, that when he answered I would get a different response. That proved to be wrong.

I hated that my mother made me relive that torture time and time again. I feel like she wanted me to paint him to be the bad guy and her, Superwoman. I already knew she was Superwoman. She was my Shero. I did not need the pain to teach me that. I can't remember him coming to one game from 2000-2010, which was basically my entire career. I do remember in high school he came to visit one time and we played catch. Again, anyone that knows me knows that I am not going to applaud a fish for swimming. But I appreciated his efforts.

You don't realize how things from your childhood affect you until you're grown. Not an adult, but grown. I didn't realize that is a huge reason why it's hard for me to ask for help. It is something that I still have to work through.

CHAPTER TWO

HIGH SCHOOL

Ninth grade comes along and we're warming up for a game. A teammate asks bluntly in front of everyone, "Hey, where's your dad? Does he ever come to games?" Insert excuse here. I don't recall what excuse I came up with, but I do remember crying. I discretely wiped the tears in between throwing and catching the ball. There awaited another shot of that fireball.

I remember being angry all over again. Why did she have to bring it up? Most importantly, why didn't he ever show up? Was he just that busy? Did he not love me? Did he hate my mother that much that he could not be there for me? I was angry, and people didn't know why. Attitude on rude. RBF on fleek. At this point, the raging emotions of a broken teenager had taken over.

I hated everything. School, softball, my family, myself.

Except for boys, I liked boys and boys liked me. I had finally graduated from a negative A-cup to an almost B-cup. I had hips, legs, and a booty. I always knew I wanted to save myself for marriage, but I was going to see how far I could go without going too far. It was a terrible game I got into, in more than one aspect of life. I played "Test the Waters". I was never good at it. In fact, if it wasn't for God, on many occasions I would have drowned.

Finally, high school boys. That was my kind of party. One could say I was fast. Every other week I called myself liking a different boy. Nothing serious. What does a high schooler know about love anyway? I was not looking for love, but a good time. That's exactly what I got. I was a complete mess. Skipping class, running rampant through the school on a fake hall pass—good times. Life was simple then. Laughing and being silly helped me forget about the deep issues I was suppressing and unwilling to tackle.

Tenth grade came along, and we got re-routed to the high school that was just built in the area. I did not want to go to this school and didn't want to leave my old friends. I wanted to stay in my comfort zone. Too bad a 15-year-old doesn't make decisions. At least not back in MY teenage days. Back to lesson one: never get used to anything. So here we go again, learning new routines, new names, new routes, everything. I particularly did not want to go to this school because I knew it would be less forgiving. But at least I had my ride-or-dies with me. Tasha and Camille. Having them made life better.

I met Tasha and Camille my 6th grade year. My family moved to a different city, and I didn't know anyone. Middle school was rough. I've never been the coolest kid, and I was going through that "awkward transitional phase." You know, when your teeth are too big for your face, and your hair is all broken off because your mom finally started letting you do it yourself. Everyone was already cliqued up, but Tasha and Camille took me under their wings. We did everything together from band to softball to sleepovers. They made life easy and pleasant. As time went on, we all went our separate ways, staying in touch from time to time. People say you don't meet your real friends until college. Although that's true, these girls were like sisters to me.

Daddy's and my relationship had been strained for a long time. I was 17–years–old and a typical teenager. I had an attitude and anger problems because of my suppression. I'd never been good at expressing my feelings verbally which is why I started writing poetry. I decided to write him a letter my senior year of high school. I poured my heart into it and let go. I decided that however he responded wasn't my problem. I just needed him to know how I'd been feeling for the past several years. I sealed the envelope and mailed it.

When he received my letter, we talked about it; he apologized and said he didn't realize that I had been feeling that way. Since then, he has put forth the effort and things are better between us. I don't feel abandoned anymore, but that came with a lot of hard work, self-searching, and forgiving. It was not an overnight process, and everything isn't always peachy between us—but what relationship is? We still have our disagreements, but I appreciate the effort he puts forth. I was glad to be heading to college on good terms.

2010

Summer of 2010 comes around and it's bittersweet. I had just graduated from high school. But my Chikae was leaving for college. Chikae was my high school boyfriend. He was an all-star football player and was headed to a D1 school. He left in July, meaning I had an entire month left until I was headed to college. I was a little insecure because I knew the college girls would be all over him. I mean, he was a sight to see...6'1, 220 pounds of pure muscle, a smile to die for, and chocolate blemish-free skin kissed by God himself. I was also feeling insecure because I had just given him a special gift. Yes, that gift. I was supposed to be saving myself for my husband. At that time, I felt that was all I had to offer. Plus, we always talked about getting married anyway, so why not? I wanted to always have my name attached to him. I knew better than to give my virginity away. It was something I prided myself on having kept for so long. I knew I was special because girls my age had already given up their gift. But I was in a bad place mentally and emotionally and needed to feel in control. So, I gave it up.

I never had anyone talk to me about sex. My mom's idea of helping me wait was telling me "Just don't do it". Maybe because my sister had a baby at 16, she shied away from the subject. Not only that, she pushed me to get on birth control in 9th grade. I did have severe menstrual cramps, and I do mean severe; birth control was known to help. On the other hand, I can't help thinking it was partly because my sister just had a baby. I remember being so curious. One time I asked my stepbrother what was sex like—he chuckled in disbelief. With him knowing that I wanted to wait until marriage, he vaguely stated, "I don't think you're going to make it." I asked "Why?" He shook his head and replied, "You're too curious." That was my sex talk. I was left to figure out everything else on my own. Television and music oversexualize everything. However, no one tells you how your emotions will change. No one explains how it opens you up to so much. Not only are you exposed to unplanned or unwanted pregnancies, sexually transmitted diseases, but also sexually transmitted "demons". Yeah, we took sex education in school, but c'mon, that's nothing compared to the real world.

I coped with Chikae's absence by working a lot of extra hours. Time was rolling on, and before I knew it, it was August. It was time to hit the road to Grambling State University, my family's alma mater. Words could not describe how I felt pulling up to campus. For the last 3 years I was at a PWI (Predominately White Institution). To give you an idea, my senior class was approximately 346 students; out of those 346 students, maybe 20 were considered African-American. To be honest, twenty is a stretch. I was the "black power" student. I'm sure my entire class hated February. I was asking all the questions and correcting the teacher, making sure they were getting the facts straight. So, when we pulled up to Grambling's campus to see all different shades of melanin, I knew I was at home. I never saw so many Black people at one time and in one place. It was truly a culture shock.

The time came for me to move my things into my dorm. My mom, my cousin, and a childhood friend who ended up at Grambling helped me move my things. Chikae was blowing up my phone. When I finally answered he went off. "Oh, you at school now and can't answer the phone?" Irritated, I responded, "You know how busy move-in day is, so don't start because I didn't do this to you." That conversation didn't last long. I wasn't about to let him ruin this day for me. I told him I would call him later after I got settled.

Finally, all moved in, I met my roommates and started unpacking. My mom said she was about to leave, and it was the first time I knew things would never be the same. See, Grambling State University is in Grambling, Louisiana—twelve hours away from my home in Charlotte, North Carolina. I knew I would never move back into the house with her and that I would only be home for some holidays. It was a rude awakening...a bittersweet moment, indeed.

We headed to the car, making last minute jokes and fighting tears. Her joke was "Ok, now you come home how you left, not pregnant." Everyone laughed, but she was so serious. She told me I was there to get a degree, not a baby. We hugged and cried and cried and hugged. It was at this moment that I realized she was my real-life best friend. I had taken all those years for granted. Time was moving swiftly, and it was hard to accept. I watched her leave as she honked the horn and waved. I went back to room 219, buried my face in my pillow and cried until my eyes were swollen and red.

CHAPTER THREE

BRIGHTER DAYS

You can't stay depressed long when it's Welcome Week. The school had an entire week planned out from comedy shows to talent shows, activities on the quad, rap battles on the yard, anything you could think of, they had it going on all day long! My roommates and I were fresh meat and we were at every activity on campus. Fun fact about me: college was when I found my passion for naps. Nevertheless, we stayed fit exercising and trying to get involved in many activities on campus. I wouldn't say we were popular, but people knew us and we knew people. Attending an HBCU is literally like gaining another family.

There is a group or organization for everyone. For me, I liked modeling, so I figured I'd join the dopest modeling troupe on campus. My roommate couldn't walk in heels and didn't want to try out. I was still interested, so I went alone.

Some older girls were there helping me perfect my "catwalk" for tryouts. I was so nervous, but I had paid the $5 audition fee, so I was going to walk like Tyra and Naomi had a baby and she was me! Tryouts went well. I made the cut! I was ecstatic about joining my first organization in college. We practiced two times a week and sometimes more if we had a show coming up. After a few weeks in, I wasn't so nervous. I was getting to know people and getting better at walking.

Feeling pretty comfortable after a few weeks and walking like I knew something, in walked this guy. He was tall, light-skinned, had light brown eyes, long hair, and a motorcycle helmet in his hand. I was like a deer in headlights. For one, I had a thing for light-skinned guys with light eyes and long hair...and the motorcycle helmet was giving me bad boy vibes, and I loved it.

He sat off to the side while we practiced, watching us. My curiosity was trying to figure out who and how important he was. We had closed practices and people were not welcomed to watch. Suddenly, people started acknowledging and speaking to him, hugging him, saying all kinds of things from "Welcome back" to "It's good to see you." **Insert grinch smile** Mister was on my radar.

When I finally got close enough, he barked, "Aye, you a freshman?" I responded with the most typical freshman answer "Why, do I look like a freshman?" With him looking unimpressed by my terrible attempt to flirt, he responded, "Yea". I laughed bashfully and answered with a shrug and nod to confirm I was, in fact, a freshman.

Practice ended and I—not so jokingly—asked him to give me a ride on his motorcycle. He said he would, but I

14

knew he wasn't going to. I let it go and told him I'd see him later. Every time I saw him at practice, I asked or—if we're being honest— nagged, "You gon' give me a ride today?" Yes, I nagged this man to let me ride his bike, don't judge me. I knew I would eventually wear him down.

After a few weeks of persistent "You gon' give me a ride today?" I reckon he finally got tired of me nagging him and annoyingly said, "Come on!" I hopped up like a little child headed to Disney World. He only had one helmet and he gave it to me. I was a little impressed. How thoughtful was that? We rode across campus to my dorm. I got off and told him, "Thank you" because I'm polite or whatever. I figured it'd be the end of our "nag-lationship" but no. He started up a conversation right there in the parking lot. We all know that parked car, parking lot conversations are the best.

We had our first real conversation. He told me he just had a birthday and turned 21. He also mentioned he just got back to Louisiana from his internship the previous semester. He told me he was about to start his senior year and that he was a double major. He seemed like a cool guy. Guess I didn't nag him too badly. I told him it was getting late and that I should get inside before the mosquitos toted me off. Before I could skate away, he asked for my number. I hated giving out my number, so I took his instead. That way I didn't have to talk to him if I didn't want to, but he was a cool guy. I walked off and I heard him say, "Aye, you gon' text me man?" With those big brown eyes, at that moment, I felt bad for him. Like, who hurt you? Smiling, I said, "Yea, I'm going to text you." I didn't have set intentions on texting him, especially because of Chikae, my boyfriend. But after he said that, I felt obligated to keep my word. So...I texted him.

It was the beginning of a new friendship. We were always laughing, making jokes, and clowning around. We started hanging out more, and he slowly became my best friend. I could and would tell him everything. It was suspicious to other people, but it was nothing because I had a boyfriend, and he had a girlfriend.

Chikae drove down to visit me early in October and things were great, couldn't have been better. I introduced him to all my friends on campus. We went on a couple of dates and enjoyed each other's time. It sucked being so far away from him. I had missed my boo-thang. We left things on great terms. He was even exploring options to get me to come visit him. The only dilemma was I didn't have a car. I didn't know anyone who would let me borrow their car for a weekend for a road trip, unlike him. I'll just say he had some really nice friends.

Late October came, I told him a male friend was coming from out of town to visit me. Well, I asked. I asked if he was ok with him sleeping on the couch. Of course, he wasn't. He was livid. He didn't like this friend, who really was just a friend. He hung up in my face and didn't answer when I called back. I called back several times, and the phone went to voicemail. I got smart and had my roommate call him from her phone, and he answered. Livid, I started going off! I probably called him every name in the book, then stormed off to my room to cool off. Spitefully, I grabbed my phone and texted Mister.

CHAPTER FOUR
THREE'S A CROWD

The day I sent that text message was the first time I admitted to myself (and only myself) that maybe I did like Mister a little more than a friend. I knew it was wrong, but I couldn't help it. Like I said before, that 'test the waters' game gets me every time. He told me he was on the yard for a parade, so I met him there. We were laughing and talking like always, getting to know one another, and probably sitting too close. A guy from the modeling troupe came up to us, spoke, then asked slyly, "Y'all talk?" Everybody on campus was nosey and had to be in all the tea. We looked at each other, laughed, and said, "No, we're just friends." A little pearl of wisdom: A lie doesn't care who tells it. He smirked like "Yea ok" and walked off.

As we sat there conversing the conversation turned into a subject of favorites. I told him my favorite food was

Mexican food, and he responded with "Yea I love some Taco Bell, too." Snorting laughing, I responded, "You do know that's not Mexican food, right?" He said, "Of course, but it just reminded me of Taco Bell...you tryna go?" I don't turn down food, so it was only right that I attended.

When I got back to my room, I was questioned on my whereabouts. Jokingly, I told my roommate I was on a date. She asked with whom, and I told her Mister. She gave me a cold stare. Uncomfortable from the ice-like glare, I kept the details to myself and got ready for bed. Her opinion mattered to me, so her cold stare bothered me. Lesson number 561: *There is always a little truth to jokes.*

November comes around and it was Bayou Classic time. My roommates and I rode the bus down to New Orleans for a weekend filled with hand grenades, Battle of the Band shows, step shows, and football. What was supposed to be an amazing time had me feeling self-conscious. It was the first time I didn't feel as close to my roommates. I felt like I was bothering them. I told myself maybe it was just me, but energy doesn't lie.

I remember being a little more reserved that weekend as I grew more uncomfortable. One roommate and I broke off from the group and hung out with my friend who attended our rival school, also known as Chikae's arch enemy. He bought our first hand grenades. Actually, our first two. He informed me that it was tradition to chug the first one. I never found any validity to that statement, but I did it for the culture.

We were on Bourbon. Lo and behold, I see Mister across the street. I went over and spoke. We had a simple conversation and parted ways. Later that night we ended up at the same club. This time when I saw him, he was loaded...so drunk that he was harassing girls. I think it actually sobered me up. I did like him, but to see him like that was a huge turn-off. I looked at him differently after that. Needless to say, he got escorted out of the club by security. Even though I was immediately unattracted to him, I still cared for him. I thought that was it. That was what I needed to see to get him out of my system. Incorrect. Later that night, I found myself calling to see if he made it ok. His brother answered the phone and let me know that he did. Annoyed and dis-appointed—yet relieved—I continued to entertain my friends as we headed to the next spot. We danced and drank all night long. It was the first time I had stayed out until the sun came up.

The next day was the football game. I felt like I had been hit by a bus, but I wasn't going to let it stop me from getting to the game. We got all dolled up, at least what I thought was dolled up at the time...because looking back at those pictures, whew child...Any-who! We got settled in and here comes a text from Mister. We linked up at the game and he was really looking like he took a hit. I asked if he was ok. He asked, "What do you mean?" I started telling him every-thing and he stared at me in disbelief, telling me he didn't remember any of that. "I think someone slipped something in my drink." I shrugged it off. It was the first pass of many that I gave him. The weekend came to an end, and we headed back to reality.

December

Things continued to get worse with Chikae—more arguing and less communication. We were both going home for Christmas so I told him I would see him then, but he insisted on coming to Grambling anyway. Things were just ok, not great.

I went through his phone. Yes, I know, I know...but I did. I saw that he'd been talking to and hanging around this particular young lady that I didn't like. This same young lady decided it'd be a good idea to call me from his phone at 3 AM months prior. At the time of the incident, I felt like something happened. How did she know me and to ask for me by name? She also sounded drunk. Either way, till this day, he is sticking to his day one story. "She was trying to call my homeboy whose name started with a K." After I confronted him about that, he tried to brush it off like nothing was going on, but he knew I didn't like her, nor did I want him hanging around with her. He dismissed the situation—and me—and he dropped it.

But I didn't. See, Chikae was a liar, but he wasn't that good at it. Not that he told huge lies, just dumb lies. For example, the first Thanksgiving we were together he went to go visit his ex-girlfriend and her family. When I asked him about it, he lied and told me he didn't. His ex had already tagged him in the picture on Facebook. When I asked him about the picture, he told me, "Oh that's old." However, the lie detector determined that was a lie. He had on a pair of shoes he had just bought. If you'll lie about little things, you'll lie about anything. Little lies caused me to not trust him. Now, back to the story.

I ended up getting a stomach virus that weekend. He took me to the ER in town and my roommate accompanied us. After drawing blood and giving me fluids, they left to go get something to eat. It was the first time they were alone together. It didn't bother me because I trusted her. They came back with McDonald's. The smell of fresh grease made me want to vomit all over again. The lab work came back normal, so I was discharged, and we all went back to the dorm.

Sunday came and he headed back to his school. Sad...because I knew it was slowly coming to an end. He deserved better. I wasn't treating him right. I couldn't shake Mister from my system, even though we had never messed around. I knew I was wrong for allowing myself to get close to him. We kissed, and I watched him drive away.

He treated me like a queen, he was gentle and kind. Why couldn't I just get it together? He'd always told me, "If we make it past the first year, we'll be ok." We'd already picked out the day we were getting married and everything. It was already shaky and that was just the first semester. With Mister in my system, the memories of all the laughs and good times began to fade.

Winter Wonderland

Winter break went well. I spent time with my family, and it was much needed as I had missed them so much. Chikae and I spent time together too, but it just wasn't the same. My heart was elsewhere, and I knew then that it was over. I hated this love triangle I had gotten myself into. I really wanted it to work with Chikae. He was the guy of my dreams, but I just couldn't shake this "bad boy" from my system. I thought it would fizzle out; I wanted it to fizzle out. But it wouldn't. Lesson number 258: *You cannot wait for sin or bad situations to die—you have to cut it off at the head.*

Winter break was coming to an end, and I could not wait to get back to my college shenanigans. I was ready to celebrate my 4.0 the college way, with game night and alcohol. Only thing is I arrived earlier than most students, so game night turned into just my roommate, her friend, Mister, and me. Yes, he was still around after Christmas break. It was obvious at this point that we liked each other, but I refused to admit it to anyone. I couldn't cheat on Chikae. I convinced myself I could handle our friendship...until that night when things got out of hand.

CHAPTER FIVE

THE FIRSTS

It was another game night, small and intimate. Mister, two friends, and me. One thing led to another that led to another. The next thing I knew, things had fully spiraled out of control. I was out of control. Boxed up hormones and emotions came out a hundred-fold. What happened to me? We were in my room kissing and breathing heavily. Articles of clothing led to my little twin-sized bed. We were getting to know one another, in the biblical sense. Chikae was the only person I'd slept with, but the sensation was so different with Mister. Too different. I'd never had unprotected sex, but if I had to imagine what it felt like, this was it. I know he had on the condom because I watched him pull it out and put it on. Then I remember hearing my father tell me, "Sometimes you have to reach your hand down there and make sure they still have the condom on, because these negroes will try to slip it off." Listening to my instinct, I reached for his nether region. No condom. Shocked and betrayed, I pushed him off of me.

I asked, "What happened to the condom?" His head nodded toward the floor while he was still trying to kiss me. "It's over there." There it was lying half open on the floor. Upset, I uttered, "Why would you act like you were putting it on, if you didn't?" He apologized. "I don't know, that was stupid. I'll go get you a plan B in the morning." Pregnancy hadn't even crossed my mind yet. I was more concerned by the fact that he acted like he was putting on the condom, and he deliberately deceived me. It was the first of many apologies that wouldn't mean sh...let's just say the first of many apologies. It was also the first huge red flag I missed—well, dismissed. Not only did I cheat on my boyfriend, but I was just betrayed by my best friend, in the worst way. I was starting the new year out great.

Now that I am older, I look back and wonder what I was going through emotionally that had me making so many "interesting" decisions. Not putting on the condom obviously wasn't that big of a deal to me because we continued to converse as if nothing ever happened. See, that was my problem. Ignoring problems in hopes that they'd just go away.

I remember feeling so dirty and ashamed after that night, and I fell into a dark place. I told my other roommate what happened, and she judged me off bat. I just needed a safe space and someone to talk to, but she didn't provide that. Lesson number 423: *Don't expect things from people just because you would do it for them*. I became even more reserved and turned to Mister as my safe place. We talked things over, and he assured me again that he was sorry and that it would never happen again. He said it was such a stupid thing for him to do. His reason was my boyfriend was a football player that was probably sleeping with multiple women; therefore, he could have contracted something—I'm assuming—from me. One, Chikae and I never had unprotected sex. Two, that's not why it was a stupid decision, friend. Three, I didn't have hard core proof that Chikae was cheating—just speculations from instances that previously occurred. I was offended by the statement, but I brushed it off because he was my safe place.

February came and I had two Valentines. Let me just stop you there. Yes, I was trifling. Now that we've established that, two Valentines. Mister and Chikae. Mister and I went on a double date Valentine's Day night and had a great time. I couldn't help but feel guilty, but I was in way too deep at this point.

Chikae came into town that weekend. He had gotten me perfume, a bear, candy, the whole nine. I felt so bad, lower than low, like a snake and a scoundrel. He wanted to spend time together, but I had a test to take. I told him I'd be back after I finished with class. He knew several of my friends on campus, so I knew he'd be fine.

He went and hung out with our friend from back home who also played football. I finished my test and headed over there to meet with them and he's over there drinking. We had plans for dinner and a movie. After I found out he had been drinking, I told him he wasn't driving me anywhere. I just attended a seminar about drinking and driving and took a pledge to never do it. This lady expressed to us how a drunk driver took her husband and kids from her, so I never wanted to be on either side of that situation. In his defense, it was only a shot. Heck, I probably led him to drink it with my shenanigans, but nonetheless, I wasn't getting in the car with him. Pissed off, I headed back to my dorm.

I called my cousin to come pick me up so I could vent, so we went to grab food. When I got back to my room, Chikae was nowhere to be found. He wasn't answering his phone, so I called my roommate. My roommates and I were no longer on great terms and only spoke when necessary. I still don't know what I did to offend them. She told me she hadn't seen him leave the room, so she didn't know. Aggravated and frustrated, I started venting to my cousin. He assured me he was probably fine. So, I let it go.

My quiet and reserved roommate comes out of her room and says, "Are you looking for Chikae?" I answered, "Yea, you saw him?" She replied, "Him and [My roommate] left together not too long ago...said they were going to a party." My head did a 360 and I saw red. I hate being lied to; it's probably in the top three of my pet peeves, aside from stepping on the rug outside of the shower with wet feet— and never mind that I was being a complete hypocrite. I made up my mind that I was going to put the paws on her when she got back. My cousin was trying his best to calm me down, but I was already in a state of rage. There was no calming me down. I told him to not get in the way because he wasn't going to be able to save her.

I heard footsteps come to the door, then the card slid

into the lock and the front door came open. I saw her, then him. I started going off. She scurried to her room to grab a few things and when she came out, I was ready. I was already using every swear word known to man, then I got off the couch and started to approach her. Before I could get to her, my cousin had me pinned against the fridge with my hands above my head, yelling "Just let her go, you got to calm down." I couldn't get him off of me, so she escaped the "placing of the paws". Now, I've never been in a fight before, so it's safe to say I could have gotten beaten up that day. But I was so angry at the entire situation—angry at how my life was going, how confused I was, how lost I was, how Mister slipped off the condom, how I cheated on my boyfriend for a guy who would betray me, how my roommates dumped me as their friend, how I was watching my life spiral out of control but couldn't do anything about it, and how I wasn't strong enough to make the hard decisions I needed to make. My roommate was just the person to push me over the edge. She ran out of our dorm like she was trying to qualify for the Olympics. My cousin held me back for what seemed like hours, but I'm sure it was only seconds. When I finally escaped his "keep me out of trouble" prison, I went outside to look for her to finish what I started, but she was gone with the wind.

I found Chikae resting on our balcony and decided to let him have it instead. I made a scene. People were coming out of their rooms trying to see what the hoopla was. This was before snap chat and Instagram, thank goodness, so no one was recording. We took it back to my room. I packed his stuff and put it at her door. I told him he could go sleep with her tonight. My exact words were "She got room for everybody else, I'm sure she'll find room for you too." I went to my room and cried myself to sleep.

Reminiscing, I was an utter mess. It's funny how life works. You deflect the attention from what you're doing and how you're feeling to make someone else seem like the bad guy instead of examining yourself. Thank God for growth.

The next day Chikae attended church with me. Before he left, I told him I didn't want to be together anymore. If I'm being honest, I was already gone mentally. It hurt like hell, but I couldn't stay in the place I was in. We hugged, I cried, he left. I was confused, I was hurt. I knew I didn't make the right decision. But it was a decision, nonetheless. What I was doing wasn't fair to him, Mister, or myself. He knew it was over, but he was so kind. He never called me out of my name, he just hugged me and kissed me and let me be.

The next day was rough. I knew I had to deal with the decision I'd made, especially knowing it wasn't the best decision. I was in chemistry class when my phone rang; part of me hoped it was Chikae, but it was Mister. He was checking on me, asking how my day was going. Considering I had excused myself a couple times to cry in the bathroom, I told him it wasn't that great. Of course, he asked why. I told him Chikae and I had broken up and I was upset about it. He responded, "I thought you were better than that. I can't believe you're letting that make you have a bad day. Guess I didn't really know you." I remember thinking, "Well, now I feel better, thanks for that." I thought he was my friend and that I could talk to him about these things and those feelings, but I had to suppress them after that statement. I didn't want to seem weak or disappoint him. After all, upon losing the relationship with my roommates and not spending time with my other friends on campus, he was all I had. I was not about to lose him, too. He told me to hit him up when I got done with classes for the day. He told me he had something that was going to cheer me up. Did I hit him up? Of course, I did. He was my "person".

He came and picked me up on his motorcycle, and we went riding. He always said riding helped clear his mind. I guess he figured, it'd clear mine too. I mean I did love riding, and I definitely needed a clear head. We went out to the country. He said he was going to show me how he relieved stress. I'm not an outdoors girl, so I'm looking at him like, "First of all, why do you have me out here?"

I waited as he rounded up empty bottles. He lined them up facing the deeper part of the woods. Then he says, "I'll be right back," and disappears for a few minutes. He came back with guns...ssss, yes gunsss. He loaded the AK and shot a few rounds. He looked well pleased as he hit each target. He loaded the smaller gun and said, "Your turn." I was scared, but Mama ain't raise no punk. He got behind me gripping my hands gently but tight, maintaining control. He whispered instructions and confidence in my ear. "Whenever you're ready, go ahead." *BANG* I jumped! I shot a gun! I really shot a gun! The adrenaline was insane, I was shaking all over. I actually hit one of the empty containers. I kept shooting and learned that I had a natural shot. I decided I was ready for the big boy toy. So, I asked if he could load the AK for me. He gave me very specific instructions; I think he was more scared than I was. I placed the butt on my shoulder, squinted through the rear sight, lined it up with the front sight, and locked my target. I just knew I was going to dislocate my shoulder, but I didn't care. I wanted to be a big girl. *TOWW* I shot the AK! I could hear the trap music playing in my head. I was a gangster. I did not dislocate my shoulder, fall, or lose control. I don't think I hit anything, but it didn't matter. Afterwards, I noticed that I felt better. We left the woods and rode back to campus.

A few days went by. Chikae had attempted to contact me a couple of times, but I wasn't ready to talk with him, so I ignored him. Still hurt over the break-up, curiosity finally led me to answer the phone. He told me he wanted to try again. He said that we could make it work and that he was sorry. Part of me wanted that too, but part of me couldn't forgive myself for what damage I had already done. Mister was my only friend at the time, and I knew I couldn't lose him. I wouldn't have anybody. I wasn't willing to cut him off to save the piece of the relationship Chikae and I had left. I had to let him go. I allowed myself to be angry with Chikae. It helped me cope with or suppress my feelings. Truth be told, I don't know that I ever got over him. Once you love someone, truly love someone, does that ever go away?

February 2011

My grandmother had been away in North Carolina for the past several months, but my mom was finally bringing her home. I had hitched a ride with my cousin to beat them to the house to make sure everything was in order for their arrival. I was checking the clock thinking they should be here any minute. I finally heard the garage door go up! Till this day, I'm like a little kid when it comes to seeing my granny and my mommy. I went outside to greet them with hugs, and that's when I saw it—a brand new shiny red car! My mom gets out and says, "Happy birthday!!" I cheesed from ear to ear. A brand new car off the lot! I couldn't wait to get back to campus. Most importantly, I gained some of my independence back.

Time continues to roll on, and I get an invitation to join a new non-Greek organization. It seemed interesting, and I figured it'd be a great way to meet new people. I went to the interest meeting which turned into the first night of the "process". I look over and see my roommate. I'm like, "Are you kidding me?" but I wasn't going to let her stop or intimidate me. To make a long story short, this is where I met Sircee. He was the line captain for the guys, and I was the line captain for the girls. We understood each other on a different level. I got along better with my brothers than my sisters.

Sircee and I were always hanging out, clowning and just being us. After we crossed, he helped me get a job on campus where he worked. We were together a lot of the time. He became one of my closest friends in college. What was I going to do when he graduated in one semester? We promised we'd stay in touch, but life happens. We ended up seeing each other every other blue moon and would catch up briefly, but that was it. I was down another friend. When you're not aligned with God, life has a way of throwing continual blows, until He has your undivided attention.

CHAPTER SIX

SUMMER 2011

I was behind a class because our nursing curriculum was too hard to follow exactly. I told myself I'd pick up two classes in the summer. I couldn't afford to pay for my classes and stay on campus because I was paying out-of-pocket. The classes were more important. I could commute from my grandma's house which was an hour away. Mister and I were discussing this, and he opened his home to me. I figured it wasn't that big of a deal because I'd been spending the night over there every night for the last few months. It was a kind gesture and saved me from getting student loans. I just had to figure out a way to hide it from my family. They're old school, so living together when you're not married...honey, please. Not to mention I was only 19 years old moving in with a 21-year-old.

We both were working, but he often left before I did.

One day I was off and decided to sleep in. I kept hearing a phone ring and, eventually, it woke me up. He had left his phone at the house that day because he was rushing for work. I sat up, grabbed it, turned it off, and tossed it across the bed. I tried to go back to sleep, but curiosity was killing me. Don't look through his phone, I told myself. Don't look through his phone, don't...too late. I beat my conscience to it. I snatched it. It's like I wasn't in control of my body. I immediately went to the text messages and started reading. Why did I have to be so curious? It was mostly our texts, a few to his homeboy, then I came across a female's name that I didn't recognize. It was a few messages back and forth. Nothing serious, but then I kept scrolling only to see Mister ask, "You wanna have sex today?" I looked at the dates and it was just a few weeks prior. While I was out pledging, he was trying to bop, knowing that I would be over that night for our nightly routine. Crushed, I just sat there. How could he? I left my boyfriend for him and this is how he acts?

I went from crushed to furious. I needed answers and he didn't get off for a few hours. I went to Facebook to do a little research. It's really convenient how the internet works. She came right up. She was light-skinned with those funny-colored eyes and a big booty. Great. Competition. I was still struggling with my complexion and self-esteem at the time. I didn't like being dark-skinned. It was always harder for us brown girls. Maybe if she was ugly, I wouldn't have been so mad. But it didn't matter because I was already furious.

I went to his brother and asked who the female was. Of course, he "didn't know" *insert eyeroll* He was his brother's keeper. We were all supposed to go to karaoke that night—Mister, his brother with his girlfriend, and I. Mister gets home, and I get straight to the point. "Who is so 'n' so?" You know a man is about to lie when he says, "Huh?" I repeated myself a little slower this time so he could have some time to think of a lie.

He says, "Oh, that's my homegirl."

Me: "Oh, we have sex with our homies now?"

Him: "What are you talking about?"

Me: "I went through your phone and saw you initiating a conversation with her about wanting to have sex. While I was on line!?!"

He dismissed the situation at hand and wanted to argue about why I went through his phone. I told him we had double date plans and to get ready.

That night at dinner he was so aggravated and angry. When we got home, he explained he was upset because I went through his phone. Flabbergasted, I just stared. "You're out here trying to thot and mad because I found out?" Unbelievable. Maybe I was wrong for going through his phone, or maybe God wanted me to see those messages. To add insult to injury, I always caught grief whenever Sircee and I would hang out. I was constantly accused of multiple things. Including getting "too dressed up" when I went to visit my grandmother, just crazy stuff. It all made sense at that moment.

He was mad for a little bit, and I suppressed my feelings about it, only bringing it up at the most convenient times. The summer went on and I passed my class, then headed home for the rest of the summer break. I was sad to be leaving Mister, but it was ok because he was going to come and visit.

I was falling in love with this man, so I wanted my mom and stepdad to meet him. I asked them if he could come visit me over the summer and they said yes! It was pretty big because he was going to stay at the house with us. Now, being old school, of course my parents didn't let us sleep in the same room; but it didn't matter I was just happy he was coming. We had a great time, and my parents really liked him. I really was starting to feel like he could be "the one."

Fall 2011

Things were going great. I was walking into my sophomore year with a 3.9 GPA and a job. I was living on campus for free because I was working for the housing department. I was on track to get into clinicals the following semester and on the road to graduating on time! Things with Mister and I couldn't have been better. Life was finally starting to look up.

I enjoyed my job. I got to meet and help a lot of people. But there was this one guy. He was older and just worked on campus from time to time. He was nice and kind of flirtatious. I liked it. We added each other on Facebook and things went from there. It wasn't anything serious, mostly laughing and joking around from time to time. Sometimes he'd come into the office and hang around my coworkers for a bit. Maybe there was a bit of spite within me from the whole text message incident with Mister months prior...or maybe it was simply a pattern that I was establishing.

Things progressed and we went from Facebook to texting. We had good conversation, but I would have to brush him off when he got inappropriate. There I was playing the 'test the waters' game. He knew I had a boyfriend, and I'm sure his intentions weren't good. But that attention, though...it would get me in trouble. I told Mister that I'd met this cool guy at work who was funny, and he flipped out. After that, I kept our relationship to myself. It got me in trouble a lot of the time because he would have to ask for me to give him information that he felt he was entitled to know.

One day the guy asked me to babysit his kid. How could I turn down the money? Mister was never one to give out money; he was quite conservative, to say the least. I had to tell Mister about it because I was actually going to this guy's house. Of course, he was upset. But hey, I needed the easy money. Nothing ever happened between this guy and me, ever. Nothing. No long hugs, kisses, etc. I could tell where he was trying to take things, so I ended up telling him we didn't need to speak any longer. This was the first "incident" Mister used to bring up and try to make it more than it was.

Once he was out of the picture things returned to normal. With the exception of classes, Mister and I did almost everything together. We went to church together and would hang out with his family all day on Sunday afterwards. I spent more time with his family than my own, even though they were only an hour up the road. We all became close. They all loved me, and I loved them. They were my people.

To wrap up 2011, it ended great. His sister had natural hair, so she was my natural hair coach and supporter. In November, I had her cut off my relaxed ends. It was a new beginning. I loved my short hair. It symbolized a lot more for me than just hair. It was a fresh start. It was getting rid of negativity. It was liberating. I felt more in control.

Out for winter break, I was riding around with my friend. The phone rings and it's my aunt. She told me I'd gotten a letter from Grambling. I said, "Is it skinny or fat?" She said "it's kind of thick." I told her to open it. She started to read the letter. "Dear Miss Bass, we would like to inform you that you've been accepted into the spring semester of clinicals..." I started screaming. I was too ecstatic. I knew my GPA dropped that semester because my workload was too much. All my teachers told me I was crazy for taking Microbiology, Pathophysiology & Pharmacology, and two other classes that semester. But I had to do what I had to do. I think I made two C's that semester. My only C's in college, but I made it. I made it.

CHAPTER SEVEN
ONLY THE BEGINNING
(JANUARY 2012)

Malachi 3:10 says, "Bring all the tithes into the store-house so there will be enough food in my Temple. If you do, says the LORD of Heaven's Armies, I will open the windows of heaven for you. I will pour out a blessing so great you won't have enough room to take in! Try it! Put me to the test!"

I had been faithful in my giving, and He was faithful to His Word. I had gotten into clinicals, but my manager didn't want to work with my new schedule, so she called a meeting with the other five employees to let them know they were going to let me go soon, then told them to not tell me. The girl that Mister's brother was dating was a good friend of mine. I even helped her get hired there. She never said a word. There I was on edge about whether I'd have a job or not. My friend knew but said nothing out of fear of losing her own job.

We had to come back to school early in order to ensure everyone's dorms were move-in ready. The week went fine. Everything was in order, and things were finished on time. Friday comes and I'm ready for a relaxing weekend. The Assistant Office Manager called me. I answered, "Hello?"

Her: "Hey, ummm, we were just calling to let you know you don't have to come back Monday. You can let today be your last day."

Me: "OK, thanks."

insert cuss words I was madder than a racist watching the 2009 presidential inauguration. I was so furious, I started fuming. These *insert derogatory noun* made me cut my winter break short to work all week just to let me go on a Friday. I was outdone. I called Mister venting and snapping. He usually made me feel better about things. I cried a little more, then I started to laugh because it was actually funny. They played me. Maybe it was one of those crazy "I should be taking medication" laughs, but nonetheless, it was a laugh.

When I told my friend I was let go, she started apologizing. Looking confused, I asked, "Why are you sorry?" She goes on to tell me, "I knew they were going to let you go, but she told us to not tell you, and I didn't want to lose my job." I punched her square in the mouth and she fell to the ground, then I started choking her...in my head. In real life, I just stood there like, "Are you serious?" Trying to be understanding, I told her she could have found a way to tell me—

drop me a hint or something. It was the first time I questioned our friendship. But life goes on. Elevation requires separation. God knew that it wasn't enough room for nursing school and that job, so I rested in that.

Life in nursing school was hardly any life at all. It consisted of studying, eating, and sleeping. In that order. Some days it was just studying. I turned 20 in February, but I can't even remember what I did for my birthday that year. I am almost sure it wasn't anything extravagant. Mister wasn't a big planner and I had ditched pretty much all of my family and friends. I'm sure I was somewhere trying to hold back tears as I read the card my mother sent. She always sent a card and a gift on my birthday. Birthdays are her thing, and she makes sure that you feel special on that day.

April 2012

It was finally starting to warm up and I was getting the hang of my nursing school load, but I missed having income. I have been working since I was 17 years old. I wasn't used to just living off refund money and savings. I asked Mister if they were hiring at his job; he told me they were. I interviewed and got the job. I was so excited. We would be working together, and I was going to be making some money. The timing was perfect because the semester was wrapping up and my job was starting in May. Everything seemed to be on the up and up, but things aren't always what they seem.

Mister and I had been doing a lot of arguing. On this particular day, Mister and I were in my dorm and we went from 0 to 100 in about 30 seconds. I honestly cannot remember what we were arguing about. He was always bringing up old news about guys and giving me grief about the way I dressed. I'm pretty sure it was about one of those two things. We were going at it, back and forth, yelling at the top of our lungs and not getting anything accomplished. I got in his face—you know, the whole index finger, mushing him, neck rolling, and cussing. He yells, "GET OUT MY FACE!", as if I was going to be like, "Yes sir", so I got even more upset. I told him that I would slap the mess out of him. He yells, "DO IT, GO HEAD, DO IT. I BET YOU WONT." Now friends, if you know me personally, you know exactly how this story ended. I felt tried, I felt challenged. "I won't do what now?" As my granny would say, I "reared back", cocked my hand, and slapped the audacity out of him. My dad always taught me, "If you hit a man, be prepared to get hit back." This man wasn't going to put his hands on.... *SMACK!*

I didn't even see it coming. It was so quick, my vision left for a second, my ears were ringing from the impact, and oh, my neck. I just held my face and started crying. He grabbed me and then it began.

"I'm sorry, my bad man." Silence filled the room. "You ok?" I said nothing. "I swear I'll never put my hands on you again." I'm crying in silence while he's begging me to speak, to say something, anything, but I had no words. The emotions I felt were all over the place. Maybe this is what I deserved for cheating on Chikae. I had no one to talk to. Even if I did, I was too embarrassed. I felt alone because he was my best friend. They say if he hits you once, he'll do it again. They say to leave after the first time because after that it just gets

41

harder. But how? Where was I going to go? The semester was almost over, and I was headed to summer school. I was already packing to come live with him while I searched for an apartment for the upcoming semester. I remember laying down and weeping myself to sleep as he apologized all night.

The next day we acted as if nothing happened and carried on with our lives. Since I knew everything, I saw no reason to leave. He wasn't going to hit me again because he had said so. Plus, it was my fault I got hit anyway. Maybe I shouldn't have made him so upset and got in his face and hit him first. Right?

Summer 2012

Things were back on track. I finished the semester with A's and B's, headed to level 2 of nursing clinicals. I started working overnight, and that was going well. I was struggling in my summer Statistics class because it was in the middle of the day. I got off work at 7 AM and class started at 1 PM. I had enough time to get home, eat breakfast, shower, and catch a few hours of sleep before class. I often did my homework at work on my break. Thank goodness my teacher and classmates were helpful. I moved in with Mister again. We decided I would stay with him until I found an apartment. Things were going well.

It was hot or cold with us. When things were good, they were great. We were best friends. We'd laugh until we cried, plan the future, read together, help each other with classes, cuddle up while watching movies, etc. There was no in-between—but as good as the good times were, the bad times were hell. It was hard because those good times were worth fighting for. We were so unstable; our foundation was shaky. The good times could turn into chaos in a matter of seconds.

We start arguing again. It seemed like the new normal. We argued about everything. This was another argument that escalated quickly. I remember being so angry that I grabbed his PlayStation and threatened to smash it. He tried me again, telling me to go ahead and do it. This time in the heat of the moment, I realized I really couldn't afford to buy him a new one, so I sat it down. Things started to get physical again, so I told him I was going to get my brothers to beat his ass if he didn't stop. Side bar: You cannot scare crazy people. He told me he would drop my brothers off in the woods— meaning kill them. I said, "You gonna kill me and hide my body too huh?!" Angry, he snapped, "Nah, that's what you'd want. I'd leave your body out for people to see." At this point, I thought, "Cool, cool, it's time for me to go." I realized this guy was really missing a few screws. So, I hit the door.

I tried to get to my car, but he was stopping me. We were outside looking like some buffoons. I was trying to get away from him, but he wouldn't let me go. I finally got in the car, locked it, and he was pulling my window down. Literally, he was manually pulling my window down. Never mind that this is my car, my new car. He was about to break my window. After I yelled at him to stop for the 100th time, he stopped only to get in front of my car so that I couldn't drive away. Now, I'm stuck because if I run him over, I'm going to jail. I can't go to jail. I'm releasing the brake and letting the car slowly go, but he's not budging. I'm hollering, "MOVE, JUST MOVE!!" After about 10 minutes of this torture, he finally moved. I turned dust leaving his driveway.

I went to Bastrop to my sister's house because I didn't know where else to go. I had to go to work that night, so I just needed to lay down and get some rest. I'm crying and visibly upset. She asked what was wrong. She's been through a similar situation, so I knew she'd understand and keep quiet. I began to tell her what happened, and I told her that it happened before. We just sat there hugging each other and crying. Hurt, she uttered, "Why didn't you tell me? You know you can always come to me. You don't have to put up with that." She was enraged. She's never wanted me to follow in her footsteps. She told me to come live with her and said I didn't have to go back. But what did I do?

I headed to work that night and arrived a little early. I sat in my car. My phone rang and it was my dad calling to check on me. We conversed for a bit, then out of the blue he asked me "Did he put his hands on you?" Shocked and angry with my sister because I knew she spilled the beans, I sat there trying not to choke on spit. This was it. Do I tell him yes or do I lie? This could be my way out; my dad could save me. I had a decision to make. As the tears took a road trip down my face, I looked over and Mister was pulling up. I choked back tears and quickly wiped my eyes. With a shaky voice and a dismissive laugh, I asked, "Why do you ask that?" He replied, "Well tell him if he does it again, I'm going to come and personally whoop his ass." I was thinking, "AGAIN?" Come whoop his ass now! I responded with, "Ok. I'll let him know."

We hung up and I called my sister, furiously asking why she would tell Daddy. She says, "I didn't tell him, I told "the mistress"—as I call her. She told the woman he left my mom for, a.k.a. his best friend. I was like, "ARE YOU SERIOUS RIGHT NOW!?! Her and I rarely speak, why are you telling my business?" She said, "I didn't know she was going to tell Daddy." At this point, I was done. I told her I had to go to work, said I loved her, and hung up the phone.

I got out of the car and Mister was waiting on me along with a million questions. After our pre-shift huddle, we hit the floor. He came to find me to start with the apologies. I ignored him. He started questioning me about why I didn't answer his texts and asking was I with "another nigga". I told him, "It's not the place or time to discuss this. We'll talk about it later." Reluctantly, he left me alone. In the morning, we headed home. Yes, I went back to his house to carry things on as if nothing ever happened. I was already in a cycle and couldn't see. Again, I figured if I just ignored the problem, it would just go away.

I went into high gear looking for an apartment because I had to get away from him. The relationship was toxic and I couldn't deal with it. He wasn't supportive at all about me moving out. He hated all of the apartments that I could afford alone. I will say that they were in bad neighborhoods, but I was willing to deal with that if I wasn't under his thumb. Then my friend (his brother's girlfriend) hits me up to tell me she thinks she may have a roommate for me. She tells me this girl is from my grandmother's hometown and that they met in class; she thinks we'd get along great. I was ready to try anything, at this point.

I added Marcia Crop on Facebook and we hit it off great! I found a little 2-bedroom/1-bathroom apartment that was absolutely perfect for us. I went to check it out with Mister, and even he liked it. I signed the lease in August, picked up our keys, and got busy moving my things out of Mister's house.

He wasn't fond of me having a roommate. He convinced himself she was going to be a hoe and have a lot of male company around me. I'm a free spirit. When I'm in the comfort of my own home, I'm wearing the minimum. Take that how you want. His concern was other men seeing me naked as if I didn't have sense enough to put clothes on if she had company. We constantly worry about things outside of our control.

Marcia and I hit it off great, we're still good friends till this day. We'd stay up late talking when we needed to be studying, talking about life and everything that came with it. Mister didn't dislike her, but he didn't like any of my friends. He trusted no one. That was another beast and round of arguments.

Fall 2012

September rolls in and I'm ready to become a big girl. Mister was still riding, and between him and my dad, they fooled around and taught me how to ride a motorcycle. What'd I do? You guessed it. I went and bought a motorcycle—a GSXR 600. It was my baby. Mister wasn't too happy about it. He said he never wanted to see me get hurt on it. He wasn't considering selling his, so that went in one ear and out the other. He had issues with me having a bike. Aside from safety reasons, he said it would draw too much attention. I mean, did he think I got it for my health? Of course not! I got it for attention and because I loved riding. He couldn't handle that and it drove him crazy.

I only had to deal with the crazy a little longer, because he was graduating in December. I think I was more excited than he was. He got two job offers: one in Louisiana and one out of state. As much as I wanted him around, I knew the out-of-town offer would be better for him, ultimately. There's not much growing one can do in Monroe, LA. Before you come for me, it's my personal opinion. So, I encouraged him to take the out of state job. We prayed over it, and it felt right. Everything fell into place from the salary he wanted to finding an apartment, then the move. The months leading up to December weren't that bad. There wasn't much arguing and no fighting. Things were actually okay.

After the graduation we packed up his apartment, packed the U-Haul, and hit the road. It wasn't too bad of a drive. He was a much better driver than I was—so he says—so he drove the entire way. Whenever we went somewhere, he didn't like for me to drive because he said I didn't pay enough attention to the road. Meh. He'd overreact to small things and dramatically put on his seat belt, then hold on to everything in the car. In my head, I'm thinking, "But did you die?" It wouldn't have been a road trip if we didn't argue. I'm telling y'all, just call us Ike and Tina. He was mad because I was sleeping. Never mind that I had worked the night before and got off at 7 AM, slept a couple hours, then helped him pack the truck. Looking back, I see he was having trouble expressing his emotions. He could have just said, "Hey, I'm getting sleepy, can we talk or play a game?" No sir, he had to cop an attitude and make smart remarks. As much as I have changed since 2012, I will say that I'm still not worth a thing on a road trip. Unless I'm driving, I go to sleep—ask Ircy and Sage. I will volunteer to ride in the back because I am zero help up front.

We finally got him settled into his new place and everything is going well again. But I had something for that. I had an attitude and started arguments over minuscule things because I was experiencing separation anxiety already. I was ready for the space because I felt like we needed it, but having to go back to school and back to a job that I was starting to hate without him was going to suck. But it was life, and I was a big girl. I was just going to have to weather it. He drove me back to Louisiana and we spent a few days together bringing in the new year. I just knew 2013 was going to be our year.

CHAPTER EIGHT

2013

    2013 was, hands down, the worst year of my life. I battled drinking, depression, loneliness, anger, guilt, frustration, abuse, you name it. We have plenty of time to get to that stuff though. Let's just start from the beginning.

    In January, I was adjusting to work and school again. I was in level 3 of clinicals and it was beyond difficult. It was Critical Care and Psychology. I couldn't even understand my Psychology teacher's accent which made the class worse. There I was working 40 hours a week, going to school full-time, entertaining a long-distance relationship, and trying to stay sane.

    I made new friends and reconnected with some old friends from freshman year. We all hung out together. By "hung out", I mean studied. Occasionally, we'd sneak off and go to the yard for ratchet activities, but it was mostly studying. We looked out for each other. I got off work at 7 AM, had classes from 9 AM to 3 PM or later. Oftentimes, I look back and don't know how I made it. It was tough and I was struggling, but I had a goal which was May 9, 2014. I had written it down; it was highlighted on my freshman year syllabus and I was sticking to it. If I fell asleep in class, they'd give me the notes from that day at our study sessions. Overall, January had 2013 looking pretty good.

February arrives and I'm looking forward to my 21st birthday! I couldn't have been more excited. My friends got me a cake and made me a nice dinner. It was kind of a big deal because nobody has ever done anything like that for me on my birthday besides my mom. I was always the one setting up surprise parties and making sure others felt special on their day. I rushed through my dinner with my friends because Mister was on his way to town and we were heading to the casino. I always chose him over everybody. He'd been gone for about six weeks, so I was ready to see him. Skyping just wasn't enough. The casino was cool, but I disliked all the smoking and I'm not a big gambler, so that was enough for me. I enjoyed my birthday spending time with him and my girlfriends, Sage and Ircy.

March sashays in bringing some interesting things. Work was blah. We had a new manager. I didn't like her. We stayed into it. It could have been my smart mouth, or it could have been because I didn't let her talk to me crazy like she did the others. We will never know. Working nights was becoming taxing, along with the demands of school and clinicals. The distance between Mister and I didn't help ease things...we started arguing more and more—mostly about my whereabouts, who I'd been conversing with, etc. It was a never-ending battle.

It was starting to warm up, so I was ready to pull Gixxer Chic back out. He definitely did not like that. One, because of all the attention I received, which I loved—and because he always told me I wasn't that good of a rider. I started riding my bike to campus parking at my old job because it was close to the building my classes were in. I was talking to some old coworkers when they introduced me to...let's call him Thing 1. He was cool. He told me he rode bikes too but recently totaled his bike in a wreck. He asked if he could ride mine. An explosive laughter escaped my soul, followed by "or nah". I told everyone bye because I had to get to class, then I walked off.

Each day that I'd park there I'd see him, and we'd talk. I told people upfront that I had a boyfriend once they got close to crossing that line. To be honest, I don't even think Mister and I were together. We had several fights and several breakups and makeups. I still told people we were together because it was less drama. I didn't have to go through the "So why are you single, why did y'all break up, aww I'm here for you" crap. At first, like a fool, I told Mister I had met this guy who rides bikes and was pretty cool. He started flipping out. In my head I'm thinking, "You aren't going to learn, are you?" I had a problem keeping my mouth shut, he was my best friend, and I wanted to share everything with him.

Thing 1 was a cool guy, and he told me he liked brown skin girls. I told him I have a friend for him and showed him pictures. He agreed that she was pretty. Feeling like Cupid, I'm prepared to bring her by to meet him. I headed to class and told her about Thing 1. She agreed to stop by and speak.

We got there and I introduced them; it was more awkward than trying to give a cat a bath. My Cupid card was revoked. She thought he wasn't interested in her, so she didn't show interest either. I kept trying, but neither of them seemed interested. That was short-lived.

It seemed like he and I talked more and more. The closer we got the more Mister started to hate him, and the more Mister started to hate him the more I liked him. Honestly, he wasn't even my type, but he was nice. He listened and didn't hurt my feelings, so that was enough for me.

One day I decided to have a kickback at my house. I invited two of my female friends, Thing 1, and my ex-coworker who introduced us. I told Mister I was having a kickback and told him who all was invited. He told me, "NO." He said that I couldn't have it and that if I did, we weren't going to be together. It was his way or the highway. I chose the highway. I was tired of him controlling every aspect of my life. I just wanted to have a little fun. It wasn't going to be anything like he expected. Except, it was everything like he expected.

Everyone arrived and we pulled out the board and card games. Everyone was laughing, joking, and having a great time. I got up to use the restroom, and a few minutes later Thing 1 showed up in the bathroom. Next thing I know, I'm on the sink breathing heavily and kissing passionately. Where did this even come from? I kept telling him—in between kisses—that we needed to stop and go back out to the living room, but the kissing never stopped. What felt like a few minutes must have been way longer than that. When we finally stopped the kissing and returned to the living room, my friend who I tried to set him up with left. I tried calling her several times, but my calls went unanswered. That was the moment I knew I messed up. I had lost Mister and my friend for some guy he tried to warn me about—but more importantly, for a guy I didn't even like.

The next day we had community service for the nursing program. It was a Race For The Cure run/walk. I saw my friend out there and tried to speak to her, but the conversation was short. I asked, "Are you going to punch me? Because I deserve it." She said, "No," and we went our separate ways.

I was so upset that day, and it wasn't any better that Mister had plans to come into town. I ran the entire race and came in first place for the girls. Fun fact about me: I used to be a jogger, especially when things upset me. Mister met me out there and I was sitting by myself. I was praying he kept the questions short because I wasn't in the mood to explain that he was right about Thing 1 liking me, and I definitely wasn't in the mood to explain that I'd just lost my friend over him. Not to mention we had just broken up for the umpteenth time the day before. I was just tired of life at this point. I was hurting, I was alone, I was broke, I was broken, I was exhausted. Between nursing school, working a full-time overnight job, and Mister, it was enough to drive anyone crazy and I had called shotgun.

Now I was dealing with doing this on my own, nursing school, and Mister. Mister and I still talked—well...argued. The more we fought the closer I got to Thing 1. Mister's verbal abuse was at an all-time high, but I was used to it. I didn't let him know it bothered me, but I internalized it and it manifested itself through unhealthy behaviors.

I used to go over and chill with Thing 1 from time to time, and we kept getting closer until one night we got too close. He didn't have protection so that was the end of that. I wasn't having unprotected sex. Point, blank, period. We continued to talk after that. After that precious sign from the Lord, I took my fast tail back over there. This time he did have condoms. Torn between this permanent decision, I didn't know what to do.

It was easier to stay than to leave. I got to know him in a biblical sense. As I lay there on my back staring at the ceiling fan I couldn't stop thinking about Mister. We weren't together, but it just didn't feel right. I didn't even like this guy like that. Questions flooded my mind, along with regret and shame. I gathered my words, then asked him to stop. I hit him with the "It's not you, it's me." In all honesty, it was me. I was using him for the company. The pain of being alone was too much, and he eased that. He wasn't even my type, but he was nice, he was funny, and he listened. He didn't make me feel bad or stupid, nor did he say hurtful things. That was enough for me. I gathered my things and left. I went home and showered, but the guilt, shame, and disgust remained intact. I promised myself I would never do that again. Sex had always been special to me, and I never wanted to minimize that.

Not long after, Mister was back in town to visit family. He ended up staying over at my house, as always. My heart was heavy, and I could not bear the burden of him not knowing. After all, he was my best friend. I had to tell him what happened. Just in case we ever got back together, I never wanted this to be something he didn't know.

I sat him down and told him I had something to tell him. He looked concerned, as he should have been. As the words "I slept with him" left my lips, tears filled his eyes. He was actually hurt. I was hurt that I hurt him. He told me he was leaving. It was late at night, so I told him that I would leave. I went to my car and sat there. With no place to go, I got in the back seat, laid down, and cried to myself. I couldn't believe this was my life. I was miserable.

After some time passed, I went back inside to continue apologizing...somehow that turned into make-up sex. We weren't together, so I don't know if that's the right term. Maybe pity sex. Whatever I could do to stop the hurt, I wanted to. We cuddled and went to sleep after that. Strange and unhealthy coping mechanisms continued to manifest.

After that, I decreased conversations with Thing 1; I would speak only when I saw him. I was upset with myself and took my anger out on him. I felt used...like he took advantage of the place I was in. He was several years older than me—at least 10. I felt like he should have known better. Now that I'm older, I fully accept responsibility. I know that I control myself and how others treat me and interact with me. Back then, I was just a young and depressed lad. That entire incident was taxing on Mister's and my broken relationship. We stayed broken up for a while.

Several months had passed. Then one night while we were skyping, he was acting like he didn't care, like he had moved on. It hurt me to my core. He was the only thing that was constant in my life. It might have been toxic, but it was reliable. I didn't want to hurt anymore. I wanted to feel the carelessness he felt, so I grabbed a shot glass. I pulled the liquor out of the freezer and told him I would just take shots until it didn't hurt anymore. I will never forget. It was the liquor to mix long islands with and it tasted terrible. At this point, it didn't matter. I poured the first one, it went down smoothly. I felt a warmth in my chest and felt a little better. Then a second...and a third...and so on, until I was crying and yelling and pouring out my feelings via Skype. Next thing I know, I'm sitting on the edge of the tub in my bathroom in the sunken place. I remember thinking, "You can end it all right now." I thought about the pills I had in the cabinet. I figured I could take them all and just go to sleep. Then, I thought about my mother and the pain she would have to endure if I made that decision. I couldn't do that to her. I had achieved my goal of feeling numb.

Startled by a thunderous knock at my door, I saw black. I heard the knock again and again. "POLICE!! OPEN UP! POLICE!! OPEN THE DOOR!" Face down on my bathroom floor, I blinked back to consciousness wondering what happened. I looked around and wondered how I ended up on the floor. Meanwhile the police were beating on my door. I gathered the strength to get up and stumbled to the door. I opened it to see the officer standing there. He asks, "Are you ok ma'am? We got a report of a fire at this address." With a confused look on my face, I looked back into my apartment to make sure there was no fire. I turned back toward the officer, and before I could speak, vomit spewed from my mouth. The officer jumped back, and I barely missed his shoes. I apologized repeatedly and cried a little. I sat in the threshold of my doorway, immensely embarrassed. He looked inside and was just as confused as I was as to why someone would report a fire. He asked if I had been drinking, as if it was not obvious. He told me to drink some water and get some rest. I sat there as the police cars and fire truck drove off.

I gathered the strength to get up from the doorstep and stumbled around until I found my phone. When I finally found it, I had several texts and missed calls from Mister asking if I was ok. I called him back and told him about the crazy event that just happened. He informed me he sent the police and fire fighters because after I passed out it looked like my apartment was filling up with smoke. To this day, I don't know if that's true or not. The only thing I can think of is maybe my breath fogged up the screen. Upset, but touched, I told him I was fine and crawled in bed.

I woke up the next morning and attempted to recall the events from the night before. It was scary. I had been drunk before, but I'd never passed out. I was all alone in my apartment that night, anything could have happened. It was the first time I thought to myself, "Maybe I have a problem." That didn't stop me from drinking, though. I didn't do drugs, so alcohol was the pain medication that I used.

Summer 2013

By the grace of God, I finished the semester strong with passing grades. But it was time for summer school, yet again. This time, I was taking Microeconomics. I still can't tell you what I learned in that class. I was just glad it was early, and I didn't have to interrupt my sleep to attend. My summer consisted of work, school, sleep, and Mister—in that order.

He and I had gotten back together for the 15,564[th] time. Our drama wasn't the main show anymore. The same friend of mine who didn't tell me I was getting fired was the same friend who kicked me out of her wedding because I wouldn't let her stylist do my hair for the wedding. But I will spare you the details of that encounter. I decided to not go to the wedding altogether because that put a strain on our friendship. Aside from that, I didn't have the money to take off work. They had already kicked the sister out of the wedding and were close to kicking Mister out too. The thing is, Mister didn't care, but I cared enough for him. I told him that weddings are stressful, even though she was being a bridezilla. I encouraged him to cooperate, because he'd end up looking back and wish he was there for his brother. I continued to encourage him to keep calm because I knew how close they were.

He coaxed me into going to the wedding anyway by saying he wanted and needed me there. It's like I was under his spell. I knew I was going to be uncomfortable, but I would have done anything for that man. He also told me he would help me out and pay me for the days I missed at work. I only made 64 dollars a night. I believe I missed 2 or 3 day. To him, that was nothing, but he was conservative with his money. Oftentimes, he let me struggle with my bills. He'd say I should be more responsible, blah, blah, blah, but we'll get to that another time.

I agreed to go to the wedding, against my better judgment. Mister had come into town and was staying at my house. We were leaving for the wedding that night because it was a long drive. I had worked the night before and went to class that morning. When I got in, we talked for a bit, but I just wanted to take a nap because I was tired. He wanted me to entertain him, give him attention, but I just wasn't up for it. He pitched a fit and said, "You know what? Fine. I hope that other nigga treating yo ass right." Now, friends, we all know by now that I have a smart mouth. I was faced with the decision to stay quiet or clap back.

Y'all know I clapped back. Upset because there was no "other nigga", I slyly replied, "Oh he is." I turned over to close my eyes for this nap I was trying to partake of, but he stormed into my room. He grabbed my legs, drug me off the bed onto the floor, then began choking me. We had several fights before this one. I mean, slapping, shoving, slamming heads against car windows, walls, pulling hair, you name it...pretty much everything except punching me in the face. Those times, I fought him back. This time I didn't care. Part of me hoped that he'd actually finished the job. My life was miserable. I laid there staring at the demon behind his eyes while he was glaring at me in disgust. I felt the grip getting tighter and breath leaving my body. I struggled for air but managed to choke out the words, "You're really going to kill me one day." He looked like he snapped back to reality and let go. I got up as if nothing happened and got back in the bed. There we were, back on the merry-go-round. Again. He started apologizing and spilling his heart. I wept to myself. He had no idea how miserable I was. Or maybe he did and just didn't care.

I slept most of the car ride; it was over a 10-hour drive. Upon arriving, it was already awkward and I'm beating myself up for even coming. It was rehearsal day. Everyone was busy like buzzing bees and I'm just trying to find a place to fit in. The wedding went well, and the weekend went by fast, so I was grateful. I was so ready to get back to Grambling, Louisiana. The ride back was awkward. Mister wanted to bring up Thing 1 again. Asking all kinds of questions like, "Was it good, was it worth it, was he more endowed than me, etc.?" With his parents in the front seats, I'm thinking this is not the time or place...can you not? But he could never "not". We had already discussed this a million times. I just wanted him to let it go. I didn't really feel like I had to even discuss it with him because we weren't together at the time that took place. Then again, I chose to tell him in the first place. I had written a poem a few days before the wedding about how I'd been feeling, explaining things. I thought it might clear some things up. I handed him my phone so he could read it. He shrugged it off as if it was nothing. I poured my heart and feelings into those words. I expressed deep dark feelings that I hid from everyone, and he brushed it off. I was so ready to get out of that car, I felt like I couldn't breathe.

Things were rocky from then on out. We had our good days. After all, we were best friends. The good days were tit for tat with the bad because we always argued over something. He talked to me like a child and often complained that I didn't listen to him. Not as in communication, but as in when he'd tell me to do something I'd always talk back. I couldn't understand why no one else saw this side of him. I battled with convincing myself that I wasn't crazy and that he was, in fact, controlling and abusive. But I did cheat on Chikae, so this was my prize. I kept telling myself I deserved this and that I didn't deserve to have a good man. He confirmed my inner affirmations with statements like, "Nobody else is going to put up with your shit, but good luck." I felt stuck.

The summer was coming to an end and my roommate had been gone all summer. Nothing unusual. I hit her up to check on her since she just graduated. She told me that she was moving out soon and that she would help pay the bills until August, but afterwards she would be gone. Devastated, I got a grip fast. At this point, I'm wondering how I'm going to pay the bills. I was just getting by with her paying half. How was I going to survive paying double?

Mister had a good paying job—I mean very good paying. He could have paid my bills, his bills, and had money left over to save. Of course, I didn't ask him to do that. I did expect more help from him financially because he was making four times more than I was. He would send a little money here and there to help out. He'd also send $40.00 for gas when I would travel to go see him. I broke down and asked him to help me with the electric bill one time. I didn't like to ask for help because I usually got a spiel on how I was eating out too much. He didn't realize it was cheaper for me to get two items off the dollar menu than to go grocery shopping.

I always had to hear about how I needed to be more responsible with my money. Never mind the facts, though. I had investments in the stock market, and I paid for the last three years of summer school sessions out of my pocket. When my bills were paid, he always wondered how I made ends meet. He would ask if men had given me money to pay bills. I look back now and don't know how I made it either. I know I struggled, but I never stopped paying my tithes. My dad sent me $125.00 a month to help out, but outside of that I never asked my parents for money. I never let them know I was struggling. I didn't want them to worry or stress about me. They had their own lives. I was a big girl and could handle this.

The months roll by after Marcia is gone and I'm struggling big time to make ends meet, keep my grades up, and keep my sanity. I was expressing my financial hardships to Mister, yet again, and he never offered me a penny to help out. Lesson number 124: *Closed mouths don't get fed.*

I told him it was extremely taxing working full time, going to class, and attending clinicals. I told him that something was going to have to give and that I might have to quit my job in a few months, and live off of my refund through May 2014. He told me he would prefer I work at night because at least he would know where I was—insinuating that I would be out doing who knows what if I wasn't working. I was stunned and hurt that the love of my life would rather I struggle than help me out so that he could know I wasn't off somewhere doing something I had no business doing. It hurt even more because I held him down while he was in school. I helped with bills when I lived with him; he even asked to borrow a hundred dollars once and I gave it to him. Before he could pay me back, he was spending money on "toys". When confronted, he got upset about it, so I let it go because at that time I wasn't pressed for money and wasn't up for the argument. He eventually ended up paying me back. My, how the tables had turned. I will say I never had to open my wallet when we were together for movies or dinner, but to be honest, I expected that. When I had money, I spoiled him in the same way.

He started treating me like a child. One time we ordered wings, and he told me, "You better eat them all, they cost too much for you to be leaving all that meat on the bones." First of all, I'm a city girl. I'm not one of those girls that can clean a bone and suck the bone marrow out, ok? I was at the point where I was getting tired of the verbal abuse and sly remarks. So, I ate the cake.

I lost 20 pounds in college. I didn't realize it until I sent my mom a picture, which was a head shot by the way, and she replied, "You need to eat a cheeseburger with extra mayo." That's when I noticed I had lost a lot of weight. Not only did I barely have time to eat, I was broke! Naps were my meals. On top of being broke, I was stressed to the max. The depression wasn't as bad as it was in the summertime. I reckon that was because I didn't have time to focus on it. I had two semesters left and I was going to graduate on time, by any means necessary.

I stuck it out and made it to December. I only had one more semester. I was counting down the weeks. I was about to take some time off from work to get my wisdom teeth pulled. When I say, 'take off some time from work', I mean permanently. I had enough PTO to last for about 2 or 3 months, along with my upcoming refund check. That was just enough money to last me until July 2014. I had it all planned out. I chose school. That last semester was too hard—working and going to school—so I put my all into going to school.

The night before my surgery, my homegirl from work was having a kickback. Several of us from work went to the kickback and it was going great. We were laughing, joking, and having a jolly good time. *KNOCK KNOCK KNOCK* Everyone from work was already at the kickback so we're all looking at the door in confusion. In walks Mister. You could have heard a rat pee on cotton. I'm sure my face showed it. He knew I was going to the kickback, but he wasn't invited...so why did he pop up? Once we all got over the initial shock, everyone who knew him spoke, asking about his new job, wondering if he liked it. I was a bit disturbed because...who does that? He came in and sat next to me. We start having a side conversation. I asked, "How did you know what apartment it was?" My eyes scanned the room curiously trying to see who was watching as he leaned in and whispered, "I heard you, you were talking loud, so don't get quiet and shy now." At this point I was learning to pick and choose my battles. Not wanting to make a scene in front of everyone, I let it go and we enjoyed the rest of the kickback.

A few days after my surgery, we headed to Mister's house. It was a couple of hours away and the heat was broken in his car. Mind you, it was December and we were headed toward the mountains. It would have been a cold ride, but he was a smart man. He brought an adaptor and we plugged in my heating pad for warmth. I slept majority of the way, snuggling with the heating pad to keep me warm. He didn't mind, and he let me sleep. I woke up realizing that I hadn't shared and quickly offered him some of the heat. He accepted. It was moments like this that kept me going. It was those times he was so kind and gentle with me that kept me hanging on. Times like that gave me the strength to fight for us.

We spent a few days at his house because he had to work. Later that week, we were back on the road to Louisiana for Christmas. My mom and aunts came into town to celebrate the holiday with my sister, grandmother, and me. Mister came over that morning, opened gifts with us, ate, then headed to his sister's. We hugged as he was leaving, and I told him I would see him in a little bit. They were doing Christmas at her house that year. I lost track of time, so by the time I made it to his sister's house everyone was full and half asleep. He had an attitude and was being standoffish with me. At this point I'm thinking, "Here we go again...what did I do now?" He was upset because I had spent majority of the day with my family and threw him to the side. I was trying to be understanding, but it was hard. I spent just about every Sunday with his family after church, whether he was there or not. I only saw my mom two or, maybe, three times a year. I was having a difficult time trying to understand why he didn't understand that. Part of me loved the fact that he wanted to spend the holiday with me, but another part of me was completely and utterly aggravated.

CHAPTER NINE

A TURNAROUND...

(JANUARY 2014)

We decided something needed to change in our relationship. That year, instead of doing our own thing for New Years, we decided to go to church. We needed all the Jesus we could get. 2014 was going to be the year we got it together. We were leaving the past behind and moving forward.

January flew by. I was adjusting to not working and just studying. It was refreshing and immensely less stressful. My classmates and I had formed a study group and got together often at libraries, our homes, club houses, on campus—basically wherever we could all fit. We would study for hours on hand, sometimes until one or two in the morning. When the study group didn't get together, often times,

Kandi and I would do our own thing. I would spend the night or leave late a lot of the time. She and I had become a lot closer during that semester. We were cool before; I'd bring her to church with me. But that semester, I shared intimate things with her about my relationship and struggles.

Mister wasn't fond of Kandi. To be honest, he wasn't fond of any of my friends. He didn't think I was spending that much time studying. After some time, he started accusing me of being gay. He'd say things like, "Oh, you must be going to your girlfriend's house." Not only was I "talking to other nig-gas" while I was supposed to be studying, now he thought Kandi and I had relations. Kandi and I laughed about it often. I mean, good for the soul laughs. We were just trying to get degrees. One time I confided in her, telling her about our problems and she said, "I knew something was off...when I looked in his eyes, he looked crazy." Finally feeling validated, I felt relieved that someone else finally saw what I had been seeing for years. I didn't let Mister's accusations bother me because they were ludicrous. I had to crank out the last se-mester and that's all I focused on. After countless accusations and arguments, we broke up *again.*

My birthday was coming up and he was coming into town. A few months prior, I had met a cousin that I didn't know I had at Grambling. He, his friend, and I would hang out when I had a few hours to spare. It was nice having family on campus again. Mister was coming to town for Valentine's Day and my birthday. It was already planned. Even though we broke up, we still spoke every day.

My cousin asked if I wanted to go to dinner with him and his homeboy to celebrate Valentine's and my birthday.

Of course, I wanted to go! I never turned down food. Mister drove in on the night of the 14th. He told me he had something for me. I was wondering why because we weren't even together, and I definitely didn't get him anything. I told him where I was out to eat and that he could meet me there. My plan was to come outside, secure the gifts or whatever he had for me, and finish my peaceful dinner.

He pulled up and texted me, "I'm outside." I went outside to meet him and he started asking me who I was at the restaurant with because he didn't see my car. I told him I was with my cousin and his friend. He got heated. He pulls the pistol out of his car, cocks it, puts it in his waistband, and heads into the restaurant. While walking swiftly he said, "You better hope you telling the truth, 'cuz I'm gonna shoot whoever you with if you lying." He marched his unstable and mentally ill self into the restaurant and immediately found my cousin and his friend. I don't know if Black people can turn red, but aside from being angry, I was so embarrassed. When he realized it was just them, he dapped them up, then left.

It was already late, and he didn't want to head to his mom's house, so he ended up sleeping on my couch that night. I woke up early because my mom always calls me early on my birthday and wants to know if I had opened her gifts. I told her I'd call her back after I opened them. She sent me some perfume, a Victoria Secret gift card, a birthday card, and some other stuff. Mister was sitting on my bed as I was smiling, loving all the birthday gifts. He asked, "Who sent the Victoria Secret stuff?" I said "Mommy." He rolls his eyes and tells me, "It probably was one of the guys back home that dropped it off and she just put her name on it and sent it." I ignored him because it was my birthday, and that's one day that I'm not going to let anyone ruin. Furthermore, it wasn't even logical.

He started being petty trying to piss me off. He had bought me a camera two years prior and was now asking for it since we weren't together. It was a gift...you don't do that. Plus, I loved that camera. I hid it at the top of my closet. He'd also bought me a ton of art supplies because I was into painting. He snatched that first and threw it in his car. We started arguing because he was taking my things. Then he started looking for the camera. He ripped my room apart looking for the camera and finally found it. I ran after him yelling to give it back because it was mine. I hopped in his car first because if we were going to play this game, then I was taking back the Polo boots I bought for him. He was faster than I was, grabbing them out of my hands, then drug me out of his car by the feet and he drove off. I went back into the house furious! Fuming mad. It was my birthday and I managed to stoop to his level letting him get me this upset. I called up Kandi and Sage to see if they wanted to go to Shreveport. I just needed to get out.

Shreveport was cool. We went shopping and went out to eat. I brought the cake Mister had bought for me so I could share with them. At the restaurant, they put candles on it, and we sang "Happy Birthday". We headed back late that night. I went home and went to bed. It was a rough birthday, but I told myself that from that year on I will strive to make myself happy. I will not wait on others to do what I would do for them. It was up to me to be happy, and I was going to make it happen.

The next day was Sunday and I was headed to church, as always. I sang in the choir, so church was a big part of my life, even though it was his family's church. That didn't matter to me because they did not know our personal business, and it was my safe place. After all, I'd been going there for 3 years, so they were my family too. After church we headed to his mom's house, as always, for family dinner. I brought the cake since we'd only eaten about two pieces. I offered the cake for dessert and Mister blurted out, "I wouldn't eat that. Ain't no telling how many niggas done picked over it." I looked at him like, "Really?" Everyone looked uncomfortable. I was tired of fighting at this point, so I just said, "Whatever." I was still upset with him about the day before and too tired to fight.

After we'd spent the majority of the day at his mom's house, we headed back to my house to "talk". We were standing outside, agreeing that it was really over this time. I told him I hope he respects his next girlfriend more and I hope that they didn't argue and fight like we did. He then proceeded to give me relationship advice on how a man should treat me. He also stated that he wasn't going to date any more dark-skinned girls or girls with daddy issues. He told me the next girl he was going to date had to be exotic looking, maybe Brazilian, or something like that. At that point, I was used to his verbal abuse. Knowing that I had daddy issues and self-esteem issues, it was a direct blow. He didn't care, he just wanted to hurt my feelings. Mission accomplished. My feelings were hurt, but it didn't break me. It just made me go harder. We hugged and said our goodbyes.

What was a goodbye to us? Nothing. It was more of a

"I'll talk to you later." We continued to converse often. I believe we both were codependent, stuck in a dead and going nowhere relationship. Time went on, and we rode the waves.

Our next biggest issue was where I was going to move after graduation. In the last semester of nursing school, you sign up to take the NCLEX (nursing boards). You have to choose a state, and that's where you register and go to take your exam to become licensed once the exam is passed.

He wanted me to take the exam in the state where he lived. I was extremely on edge about doing that. I had no family there and the way we broke up every week wasn't stable enough for me. I decided to just register in Louisiana because it was the easy option. I had been there for four years, so I might as well just stick around until things leveled out. He was upset because he wanted me to move to where he was, but I told him that wasn't happening without a ring. He told me I wasn't getting a ring without moving. Well, with both of us being headstrong, obviously, I didn't get a ring. He resented me for that, but it didn't matter to me. I was getting stronger and he couldn't handle that.

May 2014

We were still broken up, but he showed up at my graduation. I was surprised that he even came. Part of me felt like he only came so that I could never say that he didn't come. After being super supportive at the beginning of school before clinicals, then accusing me of having relations with Kandi because we studied too much, I wasn't expecting him to show his face. There he was—supporting me, regard-less.

That summer, I did quite a bit of traveling before set-tling down to take the NCLEX. Kandi and I took a road trip. We went to my hometown (Charlotte) and then to Atlanta. We were gone for a little over a week. When I got back to Loui-siana, Mister and his family planned a trip to Destin, FL. I didn't have my portion of the money to go, so Mister paid for me. He told me to consider it a graduation gift. Yes, we were still broken up at this time, but we went to Florida anyway and had a blast. 'Blast' can be defined as a good time and/or a destructive wave of highly compressed air outward like an explosion if you let the dictionary tell it. I know you're think-ing, "Huh?" Well friends, my good ol' friend Alcohol had put me in my feelings, yet again. We were having a jolly time, danc-ing and drinking at one of the local clubs. I looked over at his phone, and I see that he's been talking to this girl that he told me he wasn't talking to anymore...some little fast girl from where he stayed. Ok, she was grown, but for illustration purposes, she was a "lil girl". Anywho, she'd crossed the line before with him, so I was uncomfortable with him talking to her. He lied and said that he wasn't, but he had been. So, there I was in Florida—drunk, broke, and single with my ex-boyfriend's family in the club just shy of cussing him out. I was in my feelings. We were not even together; why was I tripping? I was trippy because he always got on me about who I was talking to. My feelings were hurt. He didn't feel like I needed any friends, let alone male friends. So here I am out of control, throwing a fit, yet again. But what did we do? If you guessed that we made up, you guessed correctly. By the time we headed home, we were back on the merry-go-round.

I scheduled myself to take boards in July. I was out of money, so I had to either pass boards or move back home. Mister was in town for a family reunion. He drove down to Shreveport with me, and we spent the night in the hotel the night before my exam. He left the next morning to get back to his family and I went into meditation. I started talking to God asking him for guidance, peace, and to help me pass this exam. I ate a small breakfast because I needed brain food. My exam was at 11 AM. I walked in, set up, and sat down at the computer. An hour later, my exam shut off after 75 questions out of a possible 265 questions. I was shocked. Nervous, but excited, I headed out the door. I went to the nearest place with Wi-Fi to see if I passed. Back then, there was a trick to it. You could try to register for the exam again and if it didn't let you, you know you passed. I tried to re-register 3 times to be sure, and I kept getting denied. I was jumping for joy! I passed my nursing boards.

I headed back to Grambling to get ready for the family reunion. I told Mister I was pretty sure that I had passed my boards. We were jumping around like some monkeys with excitement. He was there for the whole ride and I wanted to share that moment with him. I was happy that he was supportive and excited because a few days before that, it was a different story. A few days before I took the NCLEX I had been offered a full-time position at a local hospital. Uber excited, I called to tell him on the phone. He congratulated me, but he was disappointed because he wanted me to move with him. Passing the NCLEX in Louisiana and taking this job made it surreal that I wasn't moving in with him.

At the reunion, they had a talent show and I told him. I wanted to do a spoken word piece that I'd written for him. He agreed and allowed me to do so. I did my piece and won first place in the competition. It was a very good day. Times like those made me want to fight through the bad times. They were confusing. How could something so good be so bad?

CHAPTER TEN

LIFE POST COLLEGE

I didn't have any money left for rent, so in August I moved in with my friend Ircy. For a month I saved up and looked for an apartment closer to my job. I started working at the hospital and things were going well. I was loving the ER and learning so much every single day. Not to mention, the money. I had been out of work for almost 8 months. Going back to work making 3 times more than I was making and not having to go to school was amazing! Things were falling into place. I could not have been happier.

I asked my friend Sage how she liked her apartment complex and she told me she liked it a lot. I figured I'd go check it out. It was affordable and included a lot of amenities. The manager and I were riding around headed to an apartment so I could tour the inside. I saw a guy walking from his car to his apartment and he looked very familiar. I got ratchet for a second and hollered, "SIRCEE, SIRCEE!" He didn't turn around. I thought 'whoops, my bad'. Then as he turned to put the key in the door, I waved and he saw me. I asked the lady to stop so I could go talk to him. I hadn't seen him in 2 or, maybe, 3 years. We briefly caught up. I asked for a quick rundown of the apartment complex and he gave a good review. I had two friends who lived in this complex, so I took that as a sign. I took my money up there that day and signed my lease. Ircy told me I should have stayed longer to save up more, but I was used to having my own space. It would have been a smart financial decision, but no, I had to have things my way.

My life was much better. The great depression had finally lifted. Sircee and I reconnected just like old times, and Sage and I got closer. I got a gym membership and committed to working out 4-5 times a week. I had some weight to gain. I had money for groceries and was eating well. Even work was great. I loved going. Life post-college was generous.

Mister would come down and visit from time to time. The more we argued the more he pushed me away. I wasn't isolated like I was in Grambling, so I handled our fights better. The fights changed from my decision to not move to where he was to why I was getting off work so late. The thing about hospital nursing is it's shift work. Even if your relief shows up on time, you still may have to catch up on charting. Also, emergencies don't stop. There were plenty of days when traumas happened right at 6:45 PM as soon as I was about to get off. I loved being a nurse, and these people needed help, so I would stay and help out. He didn't understand that until he started shift work himself, and that's when I received an apology for his past behavior.

October comes around and I happened to be off the weekend of the Cotton Bowl. Sage invited me to come to Dallas with her and a friend. Of course, I was down to go. Another trip? I was all for it. I also knew Mister would be there with his friends and that was just extra motivation. I wanted to see him. We got all packed up and hit the road for a girl's trip. We had an amazing time from the game to the food and joking around.

Saturday night came and we were trying to find the best club in Dallas to go to. Mister and his friends were going to hit a popular club that his cousin was going to get them in. I took it upon myself to invite myself to the same club. I let him know we would be there but would be a little late. It was last minute, and the tickets were sold out, so we had to pay at the door. We arrived late, all fresh and clean, and looking good. I texted Mister and told him we were outside and asked where he was. He texted back and said, "Inside." Listen, I don't know if I was crazy or the liquor that we'd pre-gamed with in the hotel caught up with me, but I was upset. I asked him why he didn't wait for me. He told me it was because his cousin got him in. So, there we were waiting in line. I told myself to calm down and not act crazy. I begged myself to not act crazy and show out, but...I had to.

We finally got in the club and Mister told me he was by the bar. Fine, we were headed that way to get drinks an-yway. I see his group of friends and go over to them to ask for his whereabouts. They tell me, "Oh, I don't know." I laughed and applauded them for not outing their friend. I told them, "I respect that, you're your brother's keeper." Now, the sane part of me meant it, but the crazy part was ready to fight. However, I kept it together and didn't pressure them. I ordered my drink and proceeded accordingly.

I saw an old friend from my grandma's hometown in the VIP section, and he invited me and the girls to come over. We're up there partying and having a good time. I had to excuse myself to go to the restroom. As I was rounding the corner, there was Mister. Flabbergasted, I'm like, "Where have you been?" I started going off. I mean, showing out, cursing, and acting a plum fool. We'd been texting that night, but I couldn't seem to find him. There I was, out of control and trying my best to get put out of the club. After Round One ended, I headed back to VIP to cool off and regain my composure.

Text messages started coming in and Mister was asking for my location. I told him VIP. He was upset because I didn't invite him to the VIP section. I told him it wasn't my section to invite him to because I was a guest myself. Not trying to hear that, here comes Round Two. We're back to arguing. The lights finally come on and we leave the club separately.

The girls and I head to grab food after the club, then back to the hotel. Mister texts me and asks if he can spend the night. Our room was full, so he booked a room at our hotel, and I stayed with him. After a night full of arguing we weren't quite worn out, so we had to wear each other out. Yes, in that manner. They say good sex will stretch a bad relationship. We were stretched thin. We wrapped up the weekend on good terms and went our separate ways.

I was fresh out of orientation at work and nervous to

death. I was also bummed out because it was my first Sunday working. I was used to being at church every Sunday. It was a little discouraging, but I had prayed over the situation already. In walked a patient with a suit on. He told me he was a pastor and that he was supposed to be preaching, but he woke up not feeling well. After checking him out, I asked if I could ask him a question. He replied, "Sure." Back story: Mister and I always had this conversation/discussion about marriage and divorce. Neither of us believed in divorce. We agreed that once you get married, that's it. In the Bible, it says that the only reason a person can get a divorce is for fornication, according to Matthew 19:9. We agreed that married people can't fornicate, but they can commit adultery. We struggled with whether that word was interchangeable. I asked the pastor about this situation. When I tell you he read me my rights...he read me my rights. He starts telling me about my relationship with Mister and how I needed to end it. He starts telling me about my friendships, past and future. I was in tears at this point. He kept repeating, "God loves you. He loves you so much." I was sobbing uncontrollably. No one had ever prophesied over my life like that. I left the room to get myself together. It was too much to deal with at one time. God sent this man for this one lost sheep. He had his own flock to tend to, but God sent him to me because He knew I needed it. I returned with his discharge papers; his diagnosis was bronchitis. He wrote down his number, gave it to me, and told me I could call anytime I needed someone to talk to. The love I experienced from God that day was incredible.

Mister and I broke up again shortly after that conversation. He initiated it this time and I was ok with that. It was mutual. Nothing was different this time either. We still talked all day, every day. When he came into town, he still spent the night and everything. The longer we were on the merry-go-round, the meaner he became. We spun around and around and around, toying with the friendship and relation-ship lines. It was exhausting—to say the least—but it was better than being alone. He was my best friend and, after all, the good times were great. I wasn't willing or ready to give that up, even if it meant having to endure the wretched times. It wasn't that bad. At least we weren't physically fighting anymore. The rest of 2014 was on cruise control. I was focused on working, getting gains, and saving money.

CHAPTER ELEVEN

2015

Nothing spectacular was going on in January, it was just cold. I was still hitting the gym, saving lives, and adjusting to the adult life which consisted mostly of paying bills and working. Every now and then a little fun would seep through. I was getting excited because my birthday was coming up and the girls were planning a trip to Dallas for Sage and me.

Mister came to town for another visit. He met me at work to chat for a bit. I gave him the key to my place and told him I'd be home soon as I got off. He headed to my house to relax. I got a text from him that said, "You gave me the wrong key." I felt so bad and told him to come get the right one. He told me that it was ok and to not worry about it because Sircee let him in. Panicking, because there was no way he could have known Sirs [Sircee's nickname] had a key, I texted

Sirs to confirm. I asked if he let Mister in my house—which would have been totally outside of his character. He assured me that he did not and would never let anyone in without my permission. I calmed down and gathered myself before telling on myself. I asked Mister how that was possible. He told me he was kidding and was headed to see some friends and family. I told him that I would call when I got off.

Quitting time rolled around. I gave report and headed out the door dialing Mister on the way to my car. I told him he could head my way because I was en route. We talked for the entire 10-minute drive. When I got home, I kicked my shoes off at the door, like always. I went straight to the bathroom to turn on the shower, then went to my room and started stripping off my nasty work clothes. He said, "You don't pay attention." Puzzled, I responded, "What are you talking about?" I walked back to the front of my apartment to find him sitting on my couch in the dark. There was no telling how long he'd been there. Startled, I clutched my chest and I asked, "How did you get in here?" He nonchalantly replied, "Easy. I picked the lock. You need to get it changed because it is not safe." My cray-cray radar was going off, but I dismissed it, as usual, and we had a regular weekend.

I'd made excuses for Mister's behavior before, and this time was no different. I convinced myself it was my fault he had to pick my locks. Had I given him the right key it wouldn't have happened. I ran it by Sage just to be sure it wasn't a big deal. She informed me that it was a big deal, saying he shouldn't have picked my locks. She told me he was crazy for doing that. When I looked at it from her point of view, I agreed it was crazy. At the same time, I still knew if

I'd just given him the right key it wouldn't have happened. It didn't matter because nothing could stop me from being with and loving him. Even after that, nothing changed.

February sneaks up on us and it's Valentine's Day. Mister came into town, but I had to work. I left his gift out so that he could see it when he woke up. It was the newest PlayStation game at the time. I headed to work. It was a slow day, which was a nice break. My homeboy from registration came to the back to tell me I had a visitor. Looking confused, I went to the side door to see who this mystery person might be. There stood Mister, holding a huge teddy bear and other goodies. Smiling from ear to ear, I accepted his gifts. Two seconds passed and he started to question me about my homeboy up front who came to get me, asking things like, "Oh so that's your type?" Confused, I tried to answer his question, but that wasn't enough. Never mind the fact that nothing was going on. He had a live-in girlfriend and a kid. Also, I wasn't attracted to him in that manner. The conversation started to go left. I told him, "You're not about to make a scene over nothing." He left after that and I finished my shift.

After work I headed to the gym with Sircee, as always. I was finishing up on the treadmill when a wave of nausea hit me. I told Sirs I was about to go because I didn't feel good. I headed to Walmart to get ginger ale because, you know, it's a cure-all. I picked up ginger ale and saltines, then headed to my house. My energy level was decreasing fast. I finally arrived home, showered, and laid down. A few hours later, I started vomiting. I knew it, I just knew it. I felt terrible. Every 2 or 3 hours I was up vomiting and dry heaving. Mister was helpful at first, offering water and rubbing my back. In the middle of the night, I must have awakened him with my violent vomiting. He growled, "Just throw up and quit making all the noise!" I started to whimper quietly. I didn't have the energy to fight with him. He was a mean soul when he was awakened from his sleep. If I could have thrown up quietly, I would have. In that moment, in my moment of sickness, I knew it was completely over. In my heart I knew things were different. I knew he loved me, but he didn't like me. The feeling was mutual, I just wasn't strong enough to stay gone. What was the point in leaving when all it would have taken is one text to pull me back in?

The next morning, I gathered enough energy to call my job to let them know I was not coming in. I slept all day. Mister left to go get some soup for me. He tried to serve it to me, but I couldn't stay awake long enough to eat it. In and out of sleep, I heard him say, "How are you still tired and you slept all day?" Lacking the energy to explain to him how your body rejuvenates while you're sleeping, I just let it go and drifted back into sleep.

The next day I felt a little better. I wasn't as tired or nauseated. I checked my phone and had a million messages from the girls about the upcoming trip. I told them I'd been sick and was recovering. They were trying to get my opinion for the weekend because we were headed to Dallas in two days. I told them I didn't care, I just hoped that I made the trip. Mister headed back home, and I spent the next two days recovering so I could make the trip.

Friday finally came and we were ready to cut up all weekend. We packed the car and hit the road. Ircy and I picked up her friend Brielle, then headed down I-20 West to meet up with Sage and her friend. We headed to our first activity in Dallas and cut up. We were probably the only single adults there, but that didn't stop no show.

Saturday, we had to hit the mall and spend some money. We were shopping and having a jolly good time. Out of nowhere this guy comes up to me and shoots his shot. I blocked it like my life depended on it. I mean, I pinned it against the backboard and all. He went on about his business seeing that I wasn't interested. Now, all the girls were staring at me. I chuckled, "WHAT I DO?!" They knew Mister and I weren't officially together, but I was waiting on things to get better.

There we were in the middle of the mall having a come-to-Jesus meeting. These ladies gave me an intervention in the middle of the Galleria Mall. They all agreed that I deserved better and that I should leave him for good. I nodded in agreement as the tears fell down my face, but I didn't feel like I deserved better. I cheated on Chikae with this guy, and I invested four years with this guy. I didn't deserve better. He loved me, he treated me right *sometimes*. Why give that up? Nobody else was going to put up with me. I sat there and listened to all my friends who truly loved me. Yet, the enemy still won with his lies. I knew if I cut him off my life would change drastically, and I wasn't ready for that. They knew Mister before I did; heck, he introduced me to them. If he had to go, they had to go. They were my support system and I couldn't lose that. I could stand being miserable because I had been that way for so long, but lonely? I couldn't go back there. I wiped the snot from my nose and dried my reddened eyes. They hugged me and we continued shopping.

We were hitting the club that night, so we had to get right. I couldn't find anything. I left all the expensive clothes at the mall and assured the girls I had brought a freakum dress that would shut the club down. We headed back to the hotel to get some beauty rest before the turn up.

After our nap, it was like a tornado in the room trying to get five girls ready with hair, make-up, and wardrobe. I was really low maintenance. I was carrying my makeup in a Ziplock bag at the time. Yes, a Ziplock...not even a gallon size—a snack size Ziplock. I threw on some eye shadow and a little sauce on my lips. I threw on my freakum dress and told them I was ready. You could hear a rat pee on cotton when I came out to model my outfit for the girls. Hysterical laughter broke out. At that point I was confused. I was just ready to go, and these heifers are on the beds and floor laughing saying, "No ma'am, where are you going with that on?!?!" I looked down at myself, then back at them with confusion. I looked good. They stripped me down, singing old negro spirituals, taking turns clowning me. They said things like, "You look like a granny", "You look like you're going to church." They "threw the whole dress away" and made me a makeshift outfit. After an additional 30 minutes they finally approved of my outfit, we grabbed the liquor and headed downstairs to take group pictures before we sweated out hair, makeup, and outfits.

We arrived at the club and almost got kicked out before we even got in. They saw Sage throw away a container— what they "assumed" had liquor in it. It did, but they couldn't prove that. Plus, it was empty anyway. To make a long story short, we got into it with the bouncers. I don't even know how we got in, but we did. We went, we saw, we conquered, or whatever. We staggered back to the hotel and everyone crawled into bed. Not me. I had to call Mister and we had to have our daily argument about nothing. I was too exhausted to argue that night and just told him I was going to bed. The next day we headed back to Louisiana to resume our normal adult lives.

April 2015

Trying to rekindle the spark in our relationship, I suggested to Mister that he and I take a trip to Las Vegas. Neither of us had been and I thought it would be nice to get some time away from the usual. We booked the trip and headed for Sin city. We couldn't even make it through the airport without arguing. I had on some jogger pants a tank top, a cardigan, and 5-inch heels. I'd like to think I was cute. I was cute. By this time, I had been in the gym consistently and gaining weight. I was squatting deep and what do you know? I grew a booty. He was walking so close behind me he was almost stepping on the heels of my feet. I turned around and asked, "What are you doing?" He snapped back, "You wore those pants on purpose so people would look at your ass, now you walking all hard trying to make it jiggle. Ain't nobody finna be looking." Flattered and frustrated, I brushed him off.

What started off as a little rocky actually turned into a decent trip. We argued a little, but not much. That was a huge step for us. We ate good, drank good, played some games in the casino, and saw some shows. We had an amazing time. I thought to myself that maybe this was what we needed to get back on track.

May 2015

Sage asked me to go to an event with her, but I told her I couldn't go because Mister was coming into town. I could feel her eyes rolling and wondering why I was still involved with him. At the very last minute, Mister and I got into an argument, and I decided I wasn't going to spend my weekend arguing. I hit Sage up and told her to go ahead and get my ticket because I was over it. When he got into town, I told him that Sage and I had plans, but he could come over for a little while. He came over as I was getting ready. I felt the energy shift. Destined not to argue, I kept my cool and didn't ask any questions. He was livid because he drove all that way. I was ignoring the behavior which made him even more upset.

I was in the bathroom, with my Ziploc makeup bag, right, trying my best to serve a beat face. I was applying my Walmart eye shadow when he came to the door all romantic like to watch. Except it wasn't romantic at all. He pops off questions. I let out an intentional obnoxious "UGHHH I don't feel like doing this" sigh. He then asks, " Why you putting all that shit on your face?!" Mind you, my makeup is in a Ziploc bag. I literally had on eye shadow and mascara. No eyeliner, no lipstick, heck, not even foundation. I replied, "It's just eye shadow, calm down." I zipped up my makeup bag and squeezed by him to get out of the bathroom. I told him I'd be home later and would text him then. We both left the house. I headed across the street to Sage's house to spill this tea and sip on some liquor before we went to the event. The event went great and I was glad I went with her.

Sage dropped me off at home, then I texted Mister to let him know I was back. He asked if he could come spend the night. I love cuddling, so I'm like, "Sure." He got there and I told him I was about to hop in the shower. He came into the bathroom to talk to me, as usual. He asked how the event went. I told him it was nice and that I enjoyed it. He was obviously upset because I chose to go to the event over spending time with him. I didn't care, though, I was just tired of all the arguing. He was at the door messing with something. I couldn't make out what it was. Then I heard him say, "Hey, you think it would hurt if I were to tase you while you are wet?" Nervous as all get out because I knew this man was crazy, I answered nonchalantly, "Yea, probably." I couldn't let him know I was scared. He chuckled a little, like the evil chuckle. I finished showering and stepped out to dry off. He was looking at the stun gun, examining it. I watched him peripherally and tried to seem unbothered, but I got really bothered when he started walking toward me. He jumps and activates the stun gun toward me as if he was going to shock me. I yelled, "WHAT THE F*CK?!" He steps back and laughs while saying "Oh, I was just playing." I shouted, "Get out of my house!" He started apologizing, followed by saying I was overreacting. I was absolutely done. He was now certified in my book. I think he scared some common sense into me that night.

He begged and begged me to let him stay the night.

Of course, the sucker in me gave in and said, "Fine." I let him sleep on the couch, and I locked my room door. The next day as he was leaving, I told him we were done. He said he figured that. He told me I'd already been acting differently. Truth is, I was acting unbothered because the relationship was going nowhere. I was tired of the back and forth. I was trapped. I didn't have the strength to leave him for good, so I just went through the motions. I was trying to grow, and this relationship was stopping me. I knew I should have left a long time ago, but the longer you stay, the longer you are disobedient to God's instructions and the harder those instructions are to follow.

I went on with my life. I didn't date for a while because I needed to heal. We still talked pretty much everyday and that certainly wasn't helpful. Learning and establishing boundaries was hard. By June, I was determined to not get back together. I had convinced myself we could just be friends. More lies from the enemy. Time went on, we're goofing off as usual and getting along so much better. Then one day, I see a snap of him and a couple girls in a car headed on vacation. It was painful to watch. I didn't watch any more of his snaps that weekend. Later that day while scrolling on Facebook, I saw a status update of him saying,"Post a snap of you having fun and watch them not watch anymore." Super salty, I'm like really, dude? I didn't respond because it wouldn't have done any good. I internalized my anger and hurt. I should have been used to his petty posts, but I wasn't. He was always being spiteful via social media and acting like it wasn't about me when everybody and their mamas knew it was about me. After seeing that post, it was a slap in the face. It made me realize I needed to be out here living my best life as well, and that's what I did.

Brielle was the traveler and I tagged along. We—and by we, I mean she—planned a trip to Europe. In the middle of July, we went to Madrid and Barcelona. It was my first passport stamp and I had an amazing time. That's my travel buddy. I knew her, but we never hung out outside of Dallas. That trip brought us so much closer to each other. We were in Spain serving melanin, OK? . There are not a lot of dark-complected people in that part of Europe. Brielle and I are both brown-skinned with big brat doll eyes and big curly hair. Anyway, one day on the train I leaned over and whispered, "Hey, is it me, or are people staring at us?" She laughed quietly and said, "Yup" with a head nod. It was nice to be considered exotic looking for once. I felt more appreciated by those men than men in America. It was quite refreshing.

I was posting everything, and Mister...yup, he was watching my every move. We weren't talking as much then, so I couldn't understand why he was texting me, knowing I was out of the country. He was supposed to be living his best life, yet there he was on my line concerning himself with what I was doing.

We had an amazing time in Europe. We went to museums, on tours, restaurants, the beach, etc. One of the best vacations, hands down. The vacation came to an end, but our friendship and my love for traveling grew tremendously.

The end of July came around and I headed to Mister's sister's house for my niece's birthday party. Yes, her kids called and still call me "T.T.". I saw Mister there as well, but the air was a little bit different. It was stale between us. We hadn't been conversing as much but conversing, nonetheless. It was strange because when I was in Spain a few weeks prior, he was hitting me up. The communication dwindled some more, but not completely. Maybe a couple of times a week. At this point, I still wasn't ready to move on because I still loved this man. If he was going to come back and tell me he would act right, I would have been the fool to believe it.

August 2015

August made one year as a nurse and a year at my job. It was a milestone, and I was proud to save lives. I was enjoying life in every aspect. Being single was hard and there weren't many eligible bachelors in Monroe. Nonetheless, I enjoyed the peace of not having to answer to anyone.

The next week, I went home for my mom's birthday. We threw her a surprise dinner. Meanwhile, back in Louisiana, Ircy had an impromptu kickback that turned into a party. I saw Sircee snapping it up with Mister. Mister detested Sircee because he swore that we were sleeping together. Shortly after the party, Mister hit me up and said, "MAN SIRCEE IS A COOL DUDE!" I replied, "I've been telling you that, but of course you would wait until we break up to see that." Being drunk, he apologized for all the times he accused us of anything. I felt jaded that my ex and my male best friend were now cool. There were so many accusations and arguments over our friendship. Irritated, I just went to bed. I had a long weekend planned for Mama and I wasn't in the mood to be in my feelings.

Anyone who knows Mama knows she is a clown. She enjoyed her surprise dinner, but I had other things planned for the weekend as well. She'd been asking to go horseback riding for the longest. I wish y'all could see my face now. We go to the place and got loaded up on the horses. All was well, and she was loving it. We were all sitting on our horses waiting for everyone to get loaded. We started on the trail and then it started. She started hollering. Y'all!! I was almost in tears listening to my mama cut up with her hooping and hollering. In her defense, her horse was misbehaving—stopping to eat grass and galloping when he was supposed to be walking. Not to mention her reigns were too short so she didn't have much control. When he bent down, he pulled her down too. He was giving her all the grief. She was hollering, asking, "hOw mUCh LoNGeR?!" She continually said she was ready to go. Her anxiety went through the roof when a nearby runner scared another girl's horse and the horse bucked and threw her to the ground. If she wasn't already done, that put the fork in it. Never mind the fact this is exactly what she'd been asking to do. The hour and a half trail ride was over, finally. We take the horses back in, and we're toward the back of the line as far as getting unloaded. Mama starts hollering, "COME GET ME OFF THIS HORSE RIGHT NOW!!" I'm shushing her, telling her she has to wait her turn. She's just shy of cussing me out too. I've never seen her cut up in that way. Needless to say, she hated it. We got off the horses and I teased her asking if she had fun. She gave me a glare, and I erupted with obnoxious laughter and asked, "Well what you ask for it for?!?" Maybe you had to be there, but we laugh every time one of us tells this story.

We wrapped up the weekend with quality family time, which consisted of everyone sitting around watching tv and making jokes. I hated to leave, but I had to get back to Louisiana to continue adulting.

Later that month, Ircy invited Brielle and me to a party. We did it up, got a table and everything. It was her guy friend's party and he hooked us up with VIP, bottles, all of that. We were all getting ready, and this time, I did have a real freakum dress. I had graduated from a Ziploc makeup bag to an actual makeup bag with real makeup. I beat my face and sent Mister a snap saying, "When your ex out here thotting" with a smiley face. He responds, "Stop calling yourself a thot, it's not cute." He had been calling me a thot and complaining about my "thotty" behavior for years now. I was just trying to be funny, but he shut it down and I just let it go.

We arrived at the party—late, of course—only to realize it was more of an event than a party. There I stood, as my granny would say, "with all my meat out" in this freakum dress, and it wasn't that kind of party. I tugged and tugged to pull my dress down trying to not look as skimpy as I did. I rushed to our table so that my hot peach, skin-tight dress could be masked.

Her friend came over to bring a bottle. He was easy on the eyes, 6'4"-ish, nice muscular build, beautiful eyes, and was dressed to kill. I nodded my head in an approving manner when he walked away. Still not ready to move on, but I was ready for sex again. It had been a couple of months and I was headed for a dry spell. I asked Ircy for the 4-1-1 on him and she gave me what she knew. I was on board, until she told me he was abstinent and had been for years. Skrrt. Say what now? I told her never mind, I wasn't interested in that kind of behavior. I just wanted one thing and he couldn't give that to me, so he could keep his pretty self where he was.

He continuously brought bottles to our table and paid extra attention to me. I could tell he was trying to get me to notice him, but I wasn't paying him any attention. I didn't want to waste his time. He brought the bottles and I said thank you with a "hey buddy" smile, barely looking at him or making eye contact. I could tell it was eating him up. He looked like the type to always get attention and was used to getting what he wanted. The event ended and we headed back to my place to relax and get ready for another week of adulting.

I hated that I missed Ircy's party back in early August. All her kickbacks were exceptionally lit, so you can imagine my excitement when she told me she was planning another kickback. This time it was for her husband, Sircee, and Mister, since all three of their birthdays were in September. I couldn't wait. I made sure I was off that weekend, found the perfect outfit, and even planned out my hair style. I was not playing around. It had been a few months since I had sex. In fact, Mister was the last guy I had slept with, and that was back in May. I had already made up my mind that it was going down.

The weeks flew by and it was party time. I headed to Ircy's early to help set up for the shenanigans. Mister arrived early also and helped set up. He spoke in passing but that was it. I was getting groceries out of my car and he never offered to help. It was weird because he'd never let me carry groceries in the past. I peeped game, but I remained calm. He wasn't paying me any attention. I thought, "That's weird." I wondered what was going on. I pondered it as I helped prepare the food and drinks. I was going to get to the bottom of this new behavior.

The guests started arriving and I headed to go get ready for the night. The party started and the lights went out, people were cutting up dancing, drinking, and having a great time. Distracted, I was looking for Mister. He was outside on the grill slaying his title as Grill Master. I saw he was on the phone, so I stepped outside and waited until his conversation ended.

I asked him if we could talk for a second because the air between us wasn't clear and I didn't like that. He said, "Sure." He pulled the chicken off the grill and went to put it inside. He came back outside, and I asked him the usual "How have you been, what have you been up to" questions. He was very generic, as expected, playing it cool. I started inquiring about us, asking him why the vibe was different. He just looked at me. I was standing there vulnerable, waiting for an answer. Finally, he started talking. He told me how happy he had been lately. I responded, "That's great, I'm glad to hear that, you deserve to be happy."

We started reminiscing on our relationship and I told him that I missed us. He agreed and told me he missed us too. He said, "We were the "it" couple. You know people looked up to us. We would have been a power couple had we made it." I agreed we could have been a power couple, but in reality, we were two toxic people who poisoned each other. Living through the poison, that's what made us

96

stronger. People admired how strong our relationship was, but they had no idea.

We stood outside talking for at least an hour, or so, as we revisited the good times of our relationship. I started to get emotional, so I told him I was going to go back inside to the party. I started to walk away when he grabbed my arm and pulled me into his chest, then I lost it. I missed him, I missed the good times, the laughs, everything. At that moment, I dismissed the abuse and all the bad times. I could get over it if I could just have my best friend back.

After I pulled it together, we took a walk. Somehow, we ended up kissing. I'll spare all the other details. I told him we needed to stop. I didn't see us getting back together because nothing had changed, so I was questioning why we were even doing this. I headed back to the party after being MIA for over an hour and proceeded to drink a lot more. Another hour or so goes by and he falls asleep in one of the rooms. Before he fell asleep, he texted me "come here." I finally saw the text and headed to the room. This is not a sex story, so I'll be gentle with the details. However, it was one inch from going down. But he gets to asking about this guy I was conversing with. I said, "Am I asking about your boo? No, so stop asking about him." I didn't know he had a "boo", I just assumed, like he assumed with me. Meanwhile, his phone goes off, I pick it up to hand it to him and his wallpaper is his new bae.

In my head I'm thinking, WOW REALLY!!??! I showed it to him and asked, "What are you doing?" No answer. "Do you love her?" He didn't answer, so I asked again more clearly. "Do you love her?!" He replied, "I mean she's cool...yea." I sat there naked, literally and figuratively. Flabbergasted, I responded with, "You were just talking about how happy you were, so why would you mess that up? Is she your girlfriend?"

Him: "No, she's not"

Hurt, I responded, "Well, if she treats you right, why are you in my face?"

Silence fell between us. I started to put my clothes on because I wasn't a tramp. I told him to think about what he was doing and how he would feel if she was doing it to him. I told him "You know she's going to ask you what happened, and I know you're not going to lie so, yea." After I said what I thought would kill me, he kissed me again. I meant what I said, but I had a weakness for the man. I loved him so much, and I wanted him to be happy, but I wanted him to be the best man he could be for me, so we could be happy. We started going at it again. I took that as maybe they weren't all that serious.

After we messed around, we held each other like it was the end of time. In the morning, we both sobered up and said goodbye. The goodbye hug was extra long and he kissed me on my forehead. I didn't know that was going to be the official goodbye, but it was. It was time to let him go.

Less than 24 hours later, I got a notification on my phone that he changed his relationship status on Facebook to "in a relationship". It was the same girl from his phone screen. My stomach dropped into my bottom. Hurt, I cried. I was furious. I knew in my heart it was over, but that didn't help the pain. Reality checked me. I was glad that there was no chance of us getting back together, but that didn't make it any easier. I wanted him to be happy, just not yet, not that fast. I wanted him to struggle a little, like me. I wanted him to date some "no good" women. It wasn't fair. How could he move on so fast? He didn't deserve a good woman after all the hell he put me through.

There were so many emotions. I suppressed them all. I didn't let it bother me, or so I thought. I only vented to my close friends, never taking it to social media, unlike Mister. He was never the type to post lovey dovey things, but that changed. The pictures were hard enough to see, but the captions put the nails in the coffin. My friends would warn me when he posted something with a shady caption. His own sister called me one time to apologize for his immature behavior on social media. The petty captions that took shots at me did make it a little easier. I couldn't understand how he was so "happy and in love" but taking shots at me and being disrespectful. I started to feel bad for the new bae because it wasn't fair to her. I thought about reaching out to her to let her in on some things, but I didn't because it wasn't my place. If she liked it, I loved it. I wasn't at peace, but I did pray for her. I prayed that she would never have to go through what he had put me through.

A few months later, I found myself in the shower crying. I got to a point where I was screaming for God to take the pain away. It was too much to bear. I couldn't deal with suppressing my feelings anymore, I just wanted the pain to stop. I wanted to be happy and whole. But I wasn't ready. I was still angry and couldn't let go. God couldn't take it away because I held on to the anger so tightly. He wasn't going to rip it from me. He was like, "Let me know when you're ready to be healed." Sometimes, God allows us to hurt in order for us to move forward. Had Mister not gotten into the new relationship, we'd probably still be back and forth until one of us did.

Even after seeing all the shady posts, I couldn't delete him off my social media. I didn't want him to think I was salty, so I left him as a friend. Also, not a good decision. If you haven't noticed by now, I wasn't the best decision maker. I tortured myself by not deleting him as a friend and having to see his "I'm so in love with my queen who isn't a thot, who is my best friend yada ya blah blah blah" posts. If only I had been strong enough to just remove him from my friends list the band-aid wouldn't have gotten ripped off so many times.

CHAPTER TWELVE

A WHOLE NEW WORLD

(OCTOBER 2015)

I started "dating" or whatever, and that's a strong emphasis on "whatever" because it mostly was "whatever", if you know what I mean. Anyway, I was at my best friends' Sage and Ircy's homecoming. It was another "lituation". Not like the Grambling State University homecoming, but nonetheless, it was lit. There stood a 6'4" chocolate god with muscles and weight all in the right places. *Quick fun fact about me:* I am a complete sucker for tall guys. Moving along, Ircy went over to talk to him after I mentioned how fine he was. I sashayed my way over after Ircy. A complete guilty mess, I thought she hit him with the "Aye my friend wanna talk to you" but she didn't. We sparked conversationand quickly got through the interview. 1. Are you saved and love God?

2. Do you have kids? 3. Are you single? 4. Were you born a man? Sadly, you have to ask these days. 5. What do you do for a living? He passed with flying colors. I was literally melting, batting my eyes the whole nine. About to head to the game, we exchanged numbers. *insert Birdman hand rub here* It was a wrap. Your girl Ki was officially off the market. In my head. By the way, this is a no judgment zone. Now that that's clear, back to bae. I had been single for 5 months and I was ready to try again. Things were going great, we ended up at the same after party and before going home, we stood outside and conversed some more. It was cold that night, but he pulled me into his arms to keep me warm. I'm smirking over at Ircy like, "You know he's bae, right?" Never mind that I'd just met him a few hours prior. A girl knows what a girl wants. He was hypnotizing me with those big brown eyes and that beautiful smile. Dear God, it's me, Ki, again. I know I ask for a lot, but uh rum uh, can I have this one please Lord? Pretty please!

Time goes on and we exchange more conversation and each other's time. I even invited him to game night with my friends. That was kind of a big deal because I don't give everyone the pleasure of meeting the squad, but he was special to me. The effort was reciprocated. He invited me over to hang with him and his friends as well. He cooked traditional African food. Yea, I was sprung or whatever.

Things were progressing quickly, too quickly for him. He had hit the brakes so hard I was ejected from the car. When I finally woke up, I didn't know what had happened. Confusion reigned along with unanswered texts and calls. I picked up the pieces trying to figure out where I went wrong.

I beat myself up about it for a little while. One night, I was tossing and turning so I began to pray. I prayed for God to show me what happened so I could understand better for the next guy and so I could move on.

Time went by and I received a phone call. It is the 6'4 chocolate god. In a heavily masculine voice, he said, "You got a minute to talk?" Surprised, a little agitated and excited, I said, "Yea, what's up?" He came forth with a heart-filled apology. He told me that it wasn't me. His obedience to God was the answer to my prayer.

He let me know that it wasn't anything that I did. He said things were moving too fast and going too well, and he wasn't ready for that. At the time, I couldn't accept that or understand it. You order a steak, it's a great steak, but you send it back because it was too good. Nonetheless, we started back conversing from time to time, but I was over it. I was over him, or so I thought. My pride had taken control of me and wouldn't let go. I am always thinking about the future. I thought that if he leaves when things are good, then what is he going to do when we encounter rainy days? I had to move on. I didn't want to but that's what life is. When God says no, issa no.

Issa no...but what about when He is quiet? In November of 2015, Ircy and I were in the gym like we always were, eating, and chasing those gains. I never saw fine dudes in the gym. I mean they could have a nice body but 9/10 times, that was it. I stood corrected when I saw Nani. Dear gracious Lord, why did I ever have to lay my eyes on that amazon? I mean, if he wasn't my type, then I stand before you a liar.

Nani was 6'5, built big like in the 270s, bronze skin

kissed by God himself, beautiful long black locs, and pretty white teeth. You cannot tell me God didn't take His time on him. Did I forget to mention tattoos and a beard? Ircy spoke to him, and I stood there in awe like a little girl. They exchanged greetings and smiles. Meanwhile, I was standing there patiently, planning our wedding and picking out our future children's names. I snapped back to reality as we walked off and started asking her how she knew him, demanding the down-low. She is our FBI friend and is really good at getting the scoop on people.

There we were in between sets investigating his Instagram. I think these young people nowadays call it 'lurking'. Ok fine, we were lurking...Lurked out, scrolling, and comparing pictures, dates, comments, all of that. We came across what appeared to be two small chil'ins. I was like, "Welp, that was fun while it lasted." I don't do guys with kids, so it was a no for me. Kids are a blessing from God. He hadn't shared that blessing with me yet, so I didn't want to share someone else's kids. Ircy goes on to tell me those weren't his kids, but his nephews. Still uninterested, she explained and confirmed those were in fact not his chil'ins. Just like that, I was back on board. I begged her for his Snapchat since I was more active on there than Instagram. Finally, she gave it to me, and I added him. Just like Ruth, I put myself in a position to be noticed. No? Can't compare that to the Bible? OK. I made sure to snap myself in my gym clothes so he would know and remember exactly who I was. Hook, line, and sinker! A message from Nani came through.

Him: I was wondering who this was, but you're the girl from the gym

Me: Yea lol, it's me.

Him: Next time, say hello.

Me: Of course!

We exchanged more conversation throughout the day. I went out for dinner and drinks that night with some friends to celebrate a friend passing her nursing boards. We snapped all night until he told me he was going to work and then we exchanged numbers. Truth moment: This man was so fine that I didn't even interview him. Mistake number one: I let my lurking from Instagram suffice. Time goes on and I'm thinking to myself that this is too good to be true. What is he doing talking to a girl like me?! Needless to say, I put all my eggs in that basket, tied it up, wrapped it, put a bow on it, and sent it to him. This man had a career, a degree, no kids, his own car, AND a relationship with God. I was thinking any woman would be lucky...no...blessed to have this man. Why is he single?

The month went on great, we talked on the phone, texted, and hung out. He came over one night and before he left, he tried to kiss me. I pulled back and told him, "If you kiss me, you can't be kissing on other females now; I don't like to share." He leaned in further to kiss me, so I repeated myself again. Our kiss sealed the deal—or so I assumed. We weren't exclusive, but we were talking. You know, that phase where you're getting to know one another to see if you guys would make a productive couple.

For our first "date", he took me to Chick-fil-A. Anyone that knows me knows how I feel about Chick-fil-A. Tuh, ok! I thought it was weird that he paid in cash, especially since he told me he had to stop and get cash. *Fun fact about me:* I am an over analyzer, then will turn around and make an excuse for why I believe that what I believe can't be true. Lesson number 403: *Trust your gut.*

Nani confused me, but not my gut. He was sweet and overprotective at times, but distant at other times. I had a neighborhood stalker who was leaving notes on my clip by my door. When I told Nani, he got upset and asked if I was ok. I told him I was fine, just a little creeped out because this was the second time it happened. He ripped the clip down by my door so the perp couldn't leave any more notes. He told me he wished he could stay the night to make sure I was ok, but he had to work. I was sure he was feeling me then. I wasn't rushing things, but I was definitely looking forward to seeing where things could go.

Thanksgiving rolled around and I was scheduled to work. I texted my boo, "Hope you have an awesome day, don't eat too much, we have gains to get." He has a pretty big family, so it was no surprise to me when he said he had 3 houses to visit. I went on with my day, and to my surprise, he didn't offer to bring me a plate. Usually, if you like someone, or are "talking", you make sure the other is fed. Maybe it's the soft heart in me. We had offered each other food before when going out to eat, so what was different about today? Puzzled and a little disappointed, I let it go and moved on. I had a fun-filled weekend planned.

That weekend, I went to Atlanta with my homegirl Reese to visit my Pops. When I got back Nani was acting strange. There I was trying to figure out what was wrong. Typical man. He stopped answering calls and texts. I would "randomly" happen to be at the gym at the same time he was just so he would have to talk to me. We'd have casual passing conversation, but nothing like it was. I found myself puzzled as to how I could have messed this up. I was so careful. Devastated and confused, I was left trying to piece together what happened.

In December, I went on a cruise with my two stepbrothers and good friend Kandi. I, unable to let go of nothingness, allowed myself to be a headass, yet again. He asked if I would bring him back some pure white Hennessy. Of course, I was going to do it. If pure white hen would re-establish what we had, I would have brought a case back. But God. They were sold out by the time I was ready to buy them! Won't He do it, but my ole "if there is a will there's a way" head ass just had to bring him something. I grabbed some cigars and Dominican rum instead.

I got back to the States and let him know that I had a Christmas gift for him to come pick up. This negro—I mean, man—waited and avoided me for 2 weeks. Inconsiderate, at the very least. I brought you a gift and you can't even come pick it up. I was done. Six feet under, throw some dirt on it, put a rose on top. He was dead to me. I was not only angry, but hurt, because I really liked him and I cared for him. I had hopes for us. Not only that, my time was wasted, and I don't give that away freely.

Back to the prayer closet I went. Single, angry, hurt, and now bitter. "Lord, I just don't understand, did I do something? Help me to see, so I can have some peace and really, truly move on, Lord. Amen."

CHAPTER THIRTEEN
CHAPTER 24

January 1, 2016 12:01 a.m.

"SHOTS, SHOTS, SHOTS, SHOTS, SHOTS, HAPPY NEW YEAR!!!" We toasted to new beginnings, more money, and happiness. I was with my best girlfriends and as happy as I could be. We were pre-gaming at my place before we headed to the turn up. The party was lit, the liquor was strong, and the music was bumpin'. I just knew we brought the year in right. Seriously, everything that could have gone right went right in 2015, with the exception of dating. It was literally too good to me. I finally settled in at work and wasn't scared every single day. I traveled with friends. I went to Dallas, Vegas, Madrid, Barcelona, Pensacola, New Orleans, Grand Turk, and Dominican Republic all in one year! I was playing softball again. It was slow pitch, but it was so much fun. I joined a new church and finally found the strength to

leave a mentally, verbally, and physically abusive relationship. You really could not tell me anything. I was "dancing
and emphasizing", as Melanie said on "The Game" when she
got that new haircut. My hair was growing longer, booty getting wider, and money getting taller. Life was great.

The best decision I made in 2015 was to practice ab-
stinence. Yes, I know what I said before, but I'd turned over
a new leaf. I was putting the lid back on the cookie jar. Becoming abstinent, I felt liberated. I felt powerful. Now, I
thought to myself, I must be doing something right because
life was going too well.

Then came February 2016. My favorite month of all
time. Mainly because Valentine's Day is the day before my
birthday. It was unusual because I was excited about this being my first Valentine's Day alone. I needed it. I suffered from
a smidgen of codependency, so I needed to do this alone.
Although I had to work that day, it was still nothing shy of
spectacular. My friend Sircee and his girlfriend brought
M&M's and balloons for me to my job. It was a pleasant surprise. I still find it funny how God sends people right on time.

It'd been several weeks since Nani and I spoke, but I
was still lurking his Instagram, only this time at work. Yea, I
know I was a mess. A coworker comments, "I know him, is
he still engaged?" I blew it off because obviously she did not
know the man she was looking at. No way this man was engaged. I showed her another picture and she confirmed, in fact,
that this man was, if not engaged, in a long-term relationship. About 9 years to be exact, and they even lived together.
I stood there like a deer in headlights. Paralyzed with information that baffled me. How did I miss all the red flags? I
laughed out loud because God had done it again. I was outdone. I had been taken advantage of. At 23 years old I thought

I knew the game, but the game played me.

My birthday came around and I had absolutely nothing planned. That was the usual, though. Brielle and I went to the mall and spent some time together. We met up with Sage later that night and had dinner. I had dodged several phone calls from my job that day. I knew it wasn't good when they called on your off day. I needed peace on my birthday, and it was peaceful and pleasant.

Later that evening I got a message from...let's call him Kola. Remember, Ircy's 6'4" friend from the event who was bringing us bottles. Yes, him. We had been messaging back and forth from time to time getting to know one another since the end of November. Nothing serious, just casual conversation. I enjoyed conversing with him. We talked about all kinds of things. It was actually mentally stimulating which I didn't find a lot of. His message said he was sorry he missed my birthday and asked to take me to dinner one night. Surprised and flattered, I agreed. There was never anything like that between us, so to be asked to dinner was nice. It was nice to have a friend that shared the same view on premarital sex as I did. Although we were attracted to one another, the line was never crossed. There was no pressure and I never had to explain to him why I was abstinent. He just understood, and that was a breath of fresh air. Funny how the tables turn. The exact reason why I didn't want anything to do with him was now the reason I was attracted to him. After that dinner, things kind of took off. I wouldn't say we dated, but we did start spending time together when his schedule allowed.

By this time, I had learned to not put all my eggs in

one basket after Nani and The Chocolate God. I had a few on the bench, but Kola was my favorite. I was digging him a lot, but I started to notice that things had to be done on his time. He was a busy man, and I accepted that. Unintentionally, I also accepted being on the back burner. Some days we'd talk for hours, then at other times, I wouldn't hear from him for a couple of days. He confused me, and I know God is not the author of confusion.

It wasn't long before we were exchanging "pet" names. He was calling me "my heart, queen, goddess." I called him "superstar and king." There I was sliding into my pattern of falling absolutely too fast, but this time was different. He was everything I wanted in a man. He was tall, handsome, smart, educated, and spiritual. We could talk about the Bible for hours. I loved to hear him teach. He was a man of God, and men of God know how to act, they don't play with women. Meaning, I was safe in his company.

Chapter 24.2

Barely two months into the year and my life was falling apart. In February, I almost lost my job. They threatened it all the time. I stayed in the office for petty things, like talking too loudly or not getting a patient a blanket. Yes, a blanket. I couldn't even be myself at work, now pegged as "the angry black woman." Guess I shouldn't have spoken my mind as much. Nahhhh. *Fun fact about me:* I was still learning to pick and choose my battles in the corporate world, but if something isn't right, please believe, I'm going to speak up.

March creeps on in to put the icing on the cake. It was the evening of the 8th, a night I'll never forget. It rained all day long, heavy rain, no one expected it to flood. The streets were bad and getting worse by the minute. It was a terrible day at work and emotions were everywhere. You'll never forget the ear-splitting cries of a devastated mother after losing her baby. You will never forget praying, begging God to let the baby make it as you're mid-compression doing CPR. You'll never get over the doctor nonchalantly saying, "He's dead" and questioning why EMS even brought him in. And you will never remember how you held it together for the mother that lost it. All I wanted was to go home, cry, scream, and be held by my invisible boyfriend after putting away a bottle of wine.

At the shift change huddle, the hospital told us the roads were bad and offered for us to stay if we couldn't make it home. Being the determined person that I am, I was like nope, not after today. I'm going directly to the house, driving 80 in a 60...bump a ticket. I drove through the water that came to the bottom of my car door. I got to my apartment. My parking lot was flooding so I parked up the street and walked to my apartment. Thursday morning came and it was still raining, only it was more flooded than the night before. I hit a light jog to my car hoping I could float through the rain drops and not get soaked. Mission failed. I was soaked up top from the rain and the bottom from the flooded water. I looked like a mess. I got to work, borrowed some surgery scrubs and got busy.

Mid-day, Sirs called me saying my motorcycle was flooding and I needed to move it. I rushed on my "lunch" break (because what are those when you're a nurse?) to the house to find my baby halfway submerged in the water. Sirs and my neighbor moved my bike to a breezeway that wasn't flooded. I started it up to see how bad the damage was, and water shot out of the exhaust pipe like a jet ski. Devastated, I rushed back to work to finish my shift.

Friday 3.10. 2016

There was no more rain, but the water was still rising which was a mystery to the rest of my community and me. I headed to work soaked again. This time, I was smart enough to wear regular clothes and change into my scrubs once I got there. Three p.m. came, and Sage called me to say, "They are shutting off our power and doing a voluntary evacuation; if we leave, we can't come back." Now, let me tell y'all, I do this adulting thing unmedicated, so my anxiety kicks in full force at this point, and I go into panic mode. I ran and told the charge nurse that I had to go. Sage asked me if I wanted her to grab anything for me. I told her my Bible, my notebook, my scrubs, my iPad, my passport, and some underwear. I wasn't concerned about anything else, but I needed those things, at least.

Some neighbors brought their four-wheelers and chauffeured Sage through the water to my place. By the time I got there, the water was to my waist. I walked through that nasty murky swamp water to get to my apartment. I picked everything up off the floor and put it on my bed, the couch, and the countertops just in case the water came in later.

When I got off, I headed to Sage's place with Sircee.

We all lived in the same apartment complex, but I was the only one who stayed on the first floor. We agreed we would wait it out and see if they bluffed about the power. It was pretty much an adult sleepover. The power never went out that night, so we enjoyed each other's company.

Fast forward into two weeks of hell. Long story short, my apartment flooded. Thank God for a good "framily". Sage and Sircee literally held my hand through it all. Sage let me move in with her and didn't ask for money, food, anything. She told me, her house was my house (which I knew because I had a key), but at this time I needed it now, more than ever. They were there, they saw my pain, but they didn't have to go through this struggle, thank God.

They hadn't lost everything, but Talia—she got it. She was right there with me. She lost everything. She came home from vacation to nothing. To have a friend that understands and feels your pain is priceless. She asked me one day, "How are you so positive about everything? I'm glad you're taking all this well." She had no clue I was mentally wrecked.

A week later when I was able to see my place, I was devastated. My home, my comfort zone, my safe place—destroyed! I didn't know what to do. Frustrated, angry, confused, lost...words to describe me at that time. I thought about packing what little I had left and hitting I-20E until I reached home—Charlotte, NC. How was I going to put my life back together? Where do I start? What items can I save? Then I thought, thank God I have renter's insurance. Life Lesson number 234: *Renter's insurance is not flood insurance.* "I'm sorry ma'am, I wish I could help you, but we don't cover surface water damage." Devastated again. FEMA letter: "We understand that this is a tough time for you, but sorry, we're unable to approve your request for a grant. You are however, approved to apply for a loan. Feel free to appeal this decision if you think it was made in error." I was tired of hearing "Sorry, sorry, sorry." I was tired of the worrying. I was tired of the back and forth with my job about giving me the much needed time off. I was tired of watching my bank account dwindle. I was just tired.

One night I called in to my job.

Me: I was just calling to let you know I won't be at work tomorrow.

House Supervisor: Why not?

Me: My house is flooded.

Him: It just flooded? I mean, are you just finding out about it?

Me, in disbelief: Well yea, kind of, I haven't been able to return home until today.

Him: Well, you know, we really need you at work.

Me: I understand that, but my home is flooded. I'm technically homeless. I have to find somewhere else to stay, so I won't be in tomorrow.

He carelessly responded, "Well, let your charge nurse know."

Not once did he ask if I was ok or if I needed anything...nothing, nada, zilch.

Life lesson number 123,455: *Corporate America is cutthroat and does not care about you. It's about what you can do for them, not what they can do for you.*

I don't know if you've ever been mentally, physically, and spiritually tired, but I was exhausted. Two weeks after the flood, I broke down. I cried, I screamed, and I hollered at God. I was pissed, I was weak, I was hurting, I was struggling. Most importantly, I was tired of pretending like I had it all together and like it was all ok. I was tired of the stupid smile I had plastered on my face while I was drowning on the inside. My pride had been chipping away. I reached for help but received none from the government. That made me even more angry.

Many nights I worried and cried, then cried and worried. I remember the day I unlocked the door to Sage's apartment after a long day of no's and sorry's. I hung up my keys and struggled to kick off my wet rain boots at the door. I started to cry as the frustration transferred from just trying to take off my soaking boots. I clutched the wall and screamed to the top of my lungs. I was crouched over like I'd been kicked in the stomach and started screaming, and not a sissy scream either. A top of my lungs, angry, cry for help. I screamed, "YOU SAID YOU WOULDN'T GIVE ME MORE THAN I CAN HANDLE, I CAN'T DO THIS!! I AM TIRED, HELP ME, PLEASE!!!

From that moment on, things started falling in place. My church stepped up without me asking. My pastor called to check on me and said, "I didn't know you had been in a flood. I'm about to bring you a check right now." I had

116

appealed my FEMA decision two times and they finally approved it. As much as I hate to admit it, I even qualified for emergency food stamps.

By April, things were looking up. I never knew that such a devastating event could be such a blessing. You have to go through the test to get the testimony. Not only is this my testimony but being able to bless others because I went through the flood was the best part of it all. That flood was the best thing that has ever happened to me. Kola once told me, "Water is living." How could such a terrible thing that destroyed everything I had and everything I thought I was, be living? But it is. It's given life to my faith, to my mindset, and to my soul. I thought I lost everything, but all that was lost were earthly possessions. Y'all don't know when to shout. I lost all that to gain more Jesus, more wisdom, more faith, more peace, more understanding. John 4:14 says, "But whosoever drinketh of the water that I shall give him shall never thirst; but the water that I shall give him shall be in him a well of water springing up into everlasting life." Lesson 659: *Be humble or be humbled.*

May

I finally moved out of Sage's place into my own apartment. I switched to night shift at work which gave me anice raise, but it all went to my new apartment's rent. I was on the same shift as Talia and that made work so much better. It was actually tolerable. I loved working nights because it was less drama, less management, and was more peaceful. Talia loves to travel just like me. Being that we were both just flooded and lost everything, we figured we could use a get-away. Her birthday was coming up in June, so we shot for her birthday week and planned our getaway to Panama City, Panama. I was ready for another stamp!

My love life was interesting, and I don't use that term loosely. I was still abstinent, and it was going well. Kola and I started working out together, since he was training people. I loved working out with the guys showing them I could keep up. It was also time that we spent together, which was nice since his schedule was always so busy. When I showed up, his friends would say things like, "Your wife is here." Gassed up, I'd be smiling from ear to ear, shaking my head saying, "Are y'all done??"

We became pretty good friends. I was even invited over to his house when he had a get-together and met his family. I knew for sure I was in there. Guys don't just bring anybody to Mama's house, right?

It had been a few months and things were still inconsistent with him. We couldn't deny the energy, though. We never hugged for too long, kissed, or anything. We flirted here and there, exchanging words and texts that could have been taken out of context, but we never went too far. I was patient with that man because I loved him, and I wanted the best for us.

The more inconsistent he was, the more frustrated I became. He told me I was moving too fast, and he felt like I was forcing him. All I asked for was consistency. Lesson 427: *When someone is playing games with you and doesn't have good intentions for you, they get offended when you try to set boundaries.* I never asked for anything more than consistent communication. I guess that translated in his mind to, "What color scheme are we using in the wedding?" He also told me he was working on building his empire and that he wasn't ready for a queen. He said if a queen didn't have anything to do, she'd become bored. Whether or not that is hogwash will be for you to decide. All I know is God made women to be helpmates. After that conversation I started to focus lesson him. I still had a few players benched, so it was all good.

Deja Vu

Talia was a gym rat like me. After work one day, we decided to go run stadiums, but it started raining. I'm clumsy and didn't feel like getting injured, so we settled for the gym instead. We were in the gym and in walks Nani. I hadn't seen him since December. The last conversation we had was in March when he called to check on me after the flood. He called and texted a few times, but I ignored it. One day, he called, I ignored, and then he sent a follow-up text saying, "Hey, just checking on you. I see you flooded." I decided to call back and let the phone ring ONE time, then hang up, just so it could never be said that I didn't respond. The phone didn't even ring a full time before he answered. The conversation was short.

Him: Hey, how've you been?

Me: Good, you?

Him: I see you been ignoring me.

Me: OK, what's up, I saw you called.

Him: I just wanted to check on you, I saw you flooded... you good? You need anything?

Me: Uh yea I needed a place to stay but I didn't think your girlfriend was going to let me stay on the couch.

Him: Oh wow, ok. I'm surprised it took you this long to find out. How'd you find out?"

Agitated that he would fix his lips to utter those words, I said, "I didn't think so. Well, I have to go. Thanks for checking on me."

He told me to not be a stranger and we hung up. Played, I just shook my head. He hit me up one more time after that asking for nursing advice, and I gave it to him. After that, he was canceled. I had moved on. Seeing him in the gym that day totally caught me off guard. I told Talia we needed to beast out the rest of the workout because I didn't want to have to talk to him. We pushed through the rest of the workout, and I rushed to my car to avoid any interaction.

He rushed out behind us. I was almost to my car when he hollered out asking if he could talk to me for a minute. Of course, I stopped. He started by apologizing for everything, asking if I could forgive him. He told me he had cut me off because he really liked me and could see that I genuinely cared about him. He went on to say he had nothing to offer me because he was in a relationship. I told him I had already forgiven him and moved on and that he didn't have to feel bad. I told him I felt bad for him because he was stuck in a long relationship with someone he didn't seem to want to be with and allowed his good years to be wasted. He'd never looked at it like that before. He goes on to tell me that he and the girl are breaking up. I never knew there was a process for breaking up. My BS meter went off, but it wasn't worth the energy. I concluded the conversation with, "You deserve to be happy too. Just because you've done bad things in the past, doesn't mean you deserve to be miserable. I pray you find peace and solitude." He told me 'Thank you' and asked if we could start over as friends. Well, friends, this is where I put my clown wig and red nose on and told him, "Of course."

Three days later, there we were texting again. He kept apologizing trying to make up for his past behavior. I agreed to let him make it up to me by coming over to do some manly things that needed to be done around my new apartment. There I was testing the waters again. I really thought we could be "just friends".

June 2016

June 16th approached fast. Talia and I were ready for Panama. After saving lives all morning we went home, showered, and grabbed our bags. We took a couple of shots and got on the plane. We both were knocked out on the flight and woke up in the beautiful country of Panama.

When I say we let our hair down on that trip, I mean it. We had an absolute blast. We stayed in a beautiful all-inclusive resort. We went out on the town and partied, zip lined in the jungle, laid out by the pool, caught up on rest, and abused room service. It was the relax-cation and resto-ration that we both needed.

I did a lot of thinking on that trip. I decided when I got back that I was going to be done all together with Kola. Since he was so wishy-washy about answering the phone, I went old school and decided to write a letter.

We wrapped up our vacation on a good note and de-cided to return to the States to face reality again. Walking through the airport in Dallas, I saw a guy that looked so fa-miliar. We locked eyes, but I couldn't pinpoint where I knew him from. He said, "Uh hello, are you not going to speak?"

I responded with, "You look so familiar but I don't know where I know you from."

Him: The gym.

I laughed and said, "Oh yea, you're the guy who came up and introduced himself to me."

We sparked up a conversation for the hour we were waiting and headed back to Monroe together.

I waited a few days before adding him on Facebook. I went back and forth with Sage about if I should or not. We decided "what the heck" and I added him. I didn't reach out or send messages, though. I wasn't that thirsty. I was a little more reserved than that. I was going to put him on the team eventually, so it was no rush.

Back to Kola. I was done with his games, so I wrote the letter. I had decided to move in the upcoming months, and I wanted him to hear it from me. I met him at his job to give it to him. When I gave it to him, he started to open it. I asked him to wait until he got home, or at least until I left, but my request was denied. He confronted me about the letter right then and there. He defended his actions, and I knew then that there was nothing between us. He told me that he had been going through a lot and instead of chastising his behavior, I should have been a better friend to him. How was I supposed to know he was going through a rough patch when he never told me? Lesson 541: *People cannot read your mind.* Closed mouths don't get fed. If you need or want something, speak up. The conversations were sparse after that letter. He was offended and his feelings were hurt. To say the least, so were mine, so I moved on.

Although I really liked him, I was already entertaining another player, Boman. After 2015, I vowed to never put all my eggs in one basket. I kept my roster in full rotation. He was cool, he was a good friend and laid back. We'd met a couple months back, but we didn't really talk much until around this time. We were getting to know one another, but not in a biblical sense. He was simply a great guy that I was interested in getting to know on a more intimate level.

We enjoyed each other's time and conversation. I could tell he was more ready than I was, and that was challenging. He challenged me and made me realize that maybe I wasn't ready for something that serious. I tried to act "ready", but he could see right through me and called me out. The conversations eventually got shorter and shorter until they turned into just checking up on each other from time to time.

I was coming up on the end of my 2-year contract at the hospital. I knew I could not take too much more. I requested all of my PTO which stretched out to be 3 weeks. I was getting ready for vacation, and by vacation, I mean permanent vacation. The last straw was when all three managers pulled me in the office to ask me why I was talking so loud on the floor. I was appalled that they asked me why my voice was so loud instead of having the manager on the floor at the time ask me to lower my voice. They wanted to have a sit-down meeting. They complained about my attitude, as always. They pegged me as "the angry Black woman".

The conversation shifted to "Are you happy to be here? You don't seem like it, I mean, you never smile." Smiling wasn't a part of the job description, but saving lives was. They never seemed concerned about that. They never gave me compliments or told me I was doing a good job. To be honest, it was quite discouraging. Whenever I would let this get to me, I realized there was always a ram in the bush. Patients would thank me all the time, telling me, "You're so sweet" or "You're an angel", and that gave me the strength to go on.

The conversation shifted to Talia. They went on to ask me if I was leaving because Talia recently turned in her 30-day notice and they figured I wasn't far behind. I assured them that if I did not want to be here, I would not be, and they accepted it. They cracked the whip again and let me go. Little did they know, that was the exact push I needed. That "meeting" was on a Monday. I went home that same day, typed up my 30-day notice and turned it in on Friday. I slid it under my manager's door, and as soon as I did, she opened the door and asked, "What is this?". Cussing, kicking, and throwing fits in my head, I put a little air in my chest and said, "It is my resignation letter."

Appalled, she replied, "We just asked you Monday if you were thinking about quitting."

Me: Yes ma'am, I understand, but some things have come up and I am no longer able to work here full-time.

She says, "I hope everything is ok, I sure hate to lose you as a nurse."

I walked back to my car snickering to myself, knowing everything was fine. In fact, things were about to get better. I just knew she was kicking herself for approving all of my PTO at one time. Her bad. I was ready to start my vacation. Three weeks of paid vacation at that. I went back to work one more shift, ensuring I received my bonus, and then I was out of there.

July 2016

I had faith the size of a mustard seed. No, more like an apple seed. I decided to stay on PRN (as needed), just in case, but I never planned on stepping back into that place to work ever again. She must have told everyone that worked there that I was leaving. Everyone kept asking me, "Where are you going next?" They were always so nosey, always wanting to know everyone's next move. I am a private person, and seeing that saying, "Nunya bidniss" was unprofessional—and probably a little too hood for them—I just said, "I'm going to the house to sit down for a while." That was partly true. I did not have another job lined up like most people do, but I had faith, a nursing degree, and experience.

I had been talking to some travel agencies and I had a

little money saved, so I wasn't too worried about finances. I could live off of my savings for at least two months. I pretty much had it all figured out. I took my vacation and cleared my mind from the toxicity in my life. I spent time with my family and got ready for another trip.

The girls and I were headed to Puerto Rico for Brielle's birthday bash. It was, hands down, one of the best vacations of my life. The culture, the food, my friends, the beaches, the men—everything was wonderful. We lived it up. We tried new foods, drinks, went salsa dancing; you name it, we probably did it. We headed back home but stopped in New Orleans for one more night of freedom. It was two vacations in one. We were on our worst behavior the entire trip(s).

We returned home and everything was normal. I picked up my nephew and niece to spend some time with them. Sage came over to keep us company and so that I could brief her on the trip. After a long day, I put the kids to bed. Now Sage and I could really talk. I briefed her on the trip, and we exchanged laughs. I also told her I had started conversing with another guy. She was probably thinking, "Here you go again." Yeaaa, another one. We're going to call him Mr. Incognito (guy from the airport convo earlier). I had put another player on the team. I knew quite early that it wasn't going anywhere, but the conversation and his company were nice. We talked some more until it was late. She told me she was headed home, and I told her to text me when she made it into the house.

I locked up, got in the bed, and turned on my TV. *knock, knock, knock* With a look of confusion on my face, I headed to the door quietly and looked through the peep-hole. Sage was standing there with a bottle of wine. I scrunch my eyebrows with confusion and opened the door. She said "We need to talk" as she held up the bottle of wine as a sacrifice. I headed to my closet to get my black Nikes and see who we had to go fight. We headed to my room. She said, "We have something to tell you." At this point, Ircy was on the phone and says, "Mister proposed." In my heart I knew it was coming, but nothing could prepare my heart for that day. I cried a little, and as crazy as it seemed, I was relieved. I knew it was completely over between us. I appreciated that because if he would have tried to come back, I would have been back on the merry-go-round.

I suppressed all my emotions and put all my energy into myself. I never acknowledged my anger. I just ignored his shady posts and tried to move on. I was never aware of those unhealthy emotions; they manifested in different behaviors.

I started making very bad decisions as far as men. I phased Boman out. He was too good for me, and he was challenging me to face the facts. I wasn't ready for that. I was talking the talk but couldn't walk the walk. I figured that, eventually, he'd figure me out, so I cut it before it cut me. I kept Mr. Incognito around, though, for the company and the conversation. He was older than me and not really pouring anything into me. The conversation was stimulating though. We could talk about religion, different philosophies, current events—almost anything for hours. On the contrary, he was manipulative and reminded me a lot of Mister. It scared me, to be honest, but it was familiar. I knew it wasn't healthy and

I could see myself falling into a pattern, but I couldn't stop.

I was listening to a sermon once and the pastor said, "When someone comes into your life, they always make something easier, whether it be good or bad." Well Mr. Incognito made things easier for me, but not in a good way. Even though I was falling apart and spiraling out of control, I was having fun. I knew I needed to, and eventually would have to, cut him off.

I never cut a guy off without having another on deck. I decided to start phasing him out. He wasn't healthy for me to be around, so what did I do? Added another one to the roster. This time, a preacher. Help me, Father. I guess I thought talking to a preacher would help me. Nope. See, there are these things called 'root issues', and nobody can fix them but you and Jesus. You cannot depend on another person to fix you or save you. Issues I had been suppressing from the past wouldn't allow me to be great. Here we go. Travel with me into story time.

The pastor and I were getting to know one another, but not in a biblical sense. We'd met several years prior, but we both were in relationships. This time around we both were single. I was still abstinent and actually studying the Word in between cutting up. I was feeling immensely connected to God. I could hear His voice and my discernment was on point. I didn't always listen to His voice because of, well, my flesh. Anyway, I really liked him. Yes, like all the others. I thought he'd be good for me, but I never wanted to be a first lady. I never thought I was good enough for that position. God was going to have to operate, amputate, and replace if we were going that route. He was worth the try though. Not that I was looking to get married, or even in a relationship, right away, but I always asked myself, "Can I have a future with this person?"

We talked for a month solid, texting, phone calls, Facetime, all that jazz. I told him I was going to be in his city because I was visiting my cousin for her birthday. We agreed to meet up and spend some time together. I can't lie, I was a little excited. Okay, I was super excited.

I wasn't looking for a relationship, just consistency. He was certainly consistent, and I appreciated that. I texted him on my way down to see if he wanted to get together when I got there, but he told me he had plans. I understood, so I headed straight to my cousin's house to start our weekend shenanigans. Aside from getting kicked out of a restaurant for not having on "enough" clothes we had a great day. Sunday came and I invited her to come to his church with me. We went and he preached a good, 'stepping on your toes sermon', as always. After church I invited him to go to the Saints game with us. He made up some excuse and declined. Feeling a little avoided at this point, my head started to spin. He told me to let him know when I made it back to town so we could hang out.

We headed to New Orleans to see the Saints play. My cousins are huge fans. Me? Not so much. I was a Cowboys fan. I didn't talk that much trash because it was a good game, at first. Then Oakland started coming back and they got quiet. So, naturally, I had to get a couple of jokes in. It was all love, though. We enjoyed the game and headed back home. It was a Sunday. So, of course, we had to stop by Popeyes and get that good ole Sunday chicken.

We arrived back at her house, so I let him know I was back. No reply. I was headed to sleep after that good food. In comes a text asking, "What do you want to do?" I was a little aggravated at this point because I barely heard from him all weekend. Personally, I believe if someone comes to your city, you should be the one to suggest something since it's your city. In his defense, he did suggest dinner, but I already ate and was recovering from the itis. Plus, I prefer active dates— things like batting cages, gun ranges, mini golf, arcades, etc.

I was ripping through my mini suitcase trying to find something to wear. I settled on my white crop top, low cut baggy jeans, and chucks. I went to my cousin and asked her, "How do I look?" She laughed and said, "You can't wear that, you're going out with a pastor." I was standing there trying to see the problem. We weren't going to a church event; it was a private date. She shook her head and said, "You're not ready." Not understanding where she was coming from, I changed anyway to something more conservative.

He came and picked me up and we headed to the bowling alley. As soon as we got there, I headed for the bar. No shocker there. I offered to buy him a drink, but he declined because of his image. Again, I didn't understand. He asked what if one of his members saw him out there drinking. He tried to explain that it wouldn't look good. Again, I didn't understand. This time my cousin's "You're not ready" statement came to mind. Maybe I wasn't ready. My lack of understanding was a clear indication. Maybe I was still too "worldly", or maybe I just didn't care what others thought. I didn't think it was a sin to drink or wear a crop top.

We had a great time. He dropped me off at a reasonable hour and didn't even try to kiss me. He was very respectful, and it was appreciated. The next day came and I was about to head home. I didn't hear from him all day until I was about to hit the road that afternoon. It was strange that he didn't ask when I was leaving and that he didn't tell me to be careful. It was different because we usually talked all day. I brushed it off and hit the road. It was a four-hour drive, and I had a lot of thinking to do.

I marinated on what my cousin said about me not being ready, especially after the drinking conversation at the bowling alley. I overanalyzed the entire weekend on the drive back. Something just wasn't right. My overanalyzing was interrupted by a text from a friend. He told me he was going through a tough time mentally, followed by a long text about him wanting to commit suicide. I called several times, but no answer. He'd recently moved, and I didn't have his new address so I couldn't go by and check on him. I just prayed that God would be with him at that moment and that he would find a piece of hope to hold on to. I didn't know what else to do. I was numb the rest of the ride back.

CHAPTER FOURTEEN
BIRTH OF A SAVAGE

I finally got back to town and Kola hit me up. We hadn't talked much, just here and there. He asked to come by. I was lonely at the time, so I agreed. He'd been over before and nothing happened. We literally Netflix 'n' chilled, the Christian edition. I told him I was grabbing food and asked if he wanted something. Men don't turn down food, so I got him something to eat as well. He told me he was on his way. I showered and washed the weekend off me.

When he arrived, we ate and decided to start a series on Netflix. He asked if I wanted a foot massage. Of course, I did. That was nice of him, considering we'd barely been talking. There we were on the couch, relaxing and having a good time. The foot massage turned into a leg massage, then a thigh massage, then a "booty rub". I didn't mind. I had been abstinent for almost a year and a half, and it'd been a long time since

I had been touched like that. I paid it no mind because it wasn't going anywhere. He was abstinent and so was I.

It was a long and emotionally exhausting day of trying to sort my feelings out for the preacher. Plus, I tried to not be a worry-bot about a friend who was struggling mentally. I relaxed and enjoyed every sensual touch as the stress left my body. Things kept progressing and, next thing I know, we were kissing and touching. I suggested we stop. I told him he was a lot stronger than I was and he didn't really want to go there. He kept right on. I didn't have condoms because I was abstinent. Why would I have condoms? I was kicking myself. But God. The Bible talks about temptation in 1st Corinthians 10:13. "There hath no temptation taken you but such as is common to man: but God is faithful, who will not suffer you to be tempted above that ye are able; but will with the temptation also make a way to escape, that ye may be able to bear it." He'd given me a way out. No way I was having unprotected sex.

I know you're probably thinking that was the end of things. Wrong. It was only the beginning. God usually has to tell me more than once because I'm hard-headed. He'd already given me one way out, but I didn't take it.

I wanted Kola to be strong for me because I was weak at that moment. I told him I was going to the store to get condoms and if he was there when I got back, that meant he was serious. I got in the car and headed to the store, hoping he would be gone when I got back. I arrived at the gas station, and they only had Lifestyle condoms. I'm bougie so I left those bad boys right there. I got back in my car contemplating. It was late, nothing was open, and I wasn't driving across town to Walmart. Way out number two. Did I take heed?

I decided to phone a friend because I knew she would have condoms. I said if she didn't answer, it didn't need to happen. The phone rang forever, I prayed she didn't answer. Finally, "You've reached the voicemail box of..." I hung up. Great, I had an excuse to not sleep with him. Way out number three. I headed home, relieved. I wanted to sleep with him, but I didn't if that makes sense.

I pulled up and saw his car. I realized he was serious. I told him I didn't get condoms so we couldn't have sex. We sat there awkwardly for a minute, then things started heating up again. To spare the details, I'll just say it went down, raw and uncut. Halfway through, I'm in disbelief, and the conviction was so strong, I just told him to stop. He was pleased, but I was disappointed. Not in the sex, but in myself. On top of the already overwhelming day I had, I just had unprotected sex with someone who didn't even want to be serious with me. What was I thinking?

He held me after, and I started crying. Yes, I know, I know. I'm just being honest because Here Lies the Truth. He stayed a few minutes, yes, just a few—then said he had to go. It was already in the wee hours of the morning. He said he had to go home before heading to work at 6 AM, but I didn't want to be alone. I asked him to stay the night, but he said he couldn't. I asked again, practically begging. I just didn't want to be alone. He left, I locked the door, showered, and went to bed.

I never did the casual sex thing. I didn't know how it worked. Was I supposed to contact him or wait for him to contact me? Where was the rule book for this adulting thing?

I was so disappointed in myself. How did I let that happen when God gave me chance after chance after chance? I called my friend and vented. She told me it was ok and that we all mess up. It didn't make me feel any better, though. I sulked all day. The enemy whispered lies and guilt all day. I received a text from him later on that evening saying, "I've been thinking about you all day." Unimpressed and unsure of how to respond, I replied, "Oh really?" The conversation went absolutely nowhere. After that the conversation got even thinner between us, and I started to question if he was even abstinent for all those years, or if he used that to play me. Once I got over that, my savage mode was activated.

I'd never been a savage before, but it came quite naturally. The preacher dude had completely gone MIA after I got back from visiting. Savage mode 2.0 kicked in. I was headed downhill fast, but I couldn't stop myself. I had been a good girl and that got me nowhere, so why not act up? I was over the good girl act. I had already run off Boman, a really great catch, and settled for Mr. Incognito, who wasn't working, sat at home listening to music and playing video games all day. I couldn't help but think, "How in the world did I get here?"

He was so abrasive, but I kept giving him chances. One day we were hanging out at my house, and we were talking. I got up and walked away because I didn't like what he was saying. He grabbed my arm and said, "Don't walk away from me." I snatched away and started cussing him out. He didn't understand why I went from 0 to 100. He didn't know my past, but I was taken back there. I promised myself I'd never let another man put his hands on me. He said,

"What's the problem? You're acting like somebody put their hands on you before." I told him, "They have, so don't ever grab me like that again." He apologized and I fixed myself another glass of wine.

The thing with unresolved issues is they always pop back up. When you suppress them, 9 times out of 10 they're going to come back up, but maybe in different areas of your life just like the "Whack-A-Mole" game. You take one out, or so you think, and another one pops up. It could be in the same area, it could be in a different area. You could be upset about something so small because you have unresolved issues in your heart.

I let it slide, and we continued to hang out. One day we went to the park just to chill. Now, aside from him not being super productive in life at the moment, we did vibe and the conversation was always on point. Plus, he'd restored his entire house after the flood and that was super attractive to me—not to mention, he was former military. Did I mention he was 6'5? So, yea. Maybe it was infatuation, but it was a big turn on...and those were reasons that I excused his current situation. Anywho, we were in the park chopping it up and he gets abrasive again. I told him I didn't like the way he was talking to me and suggested he stop. His response was, "Would you rather me talk to you crazy or be beating your ass?" Flabbergasted, I let out an obnoxious "WWOOOOWW, REALLY?" I told him that was way below the belt. He tried to cover it up and say he didn't mean it like that, but I knew exactly how he meant it. He was super canceled from that point on. I knew I'd keep him around for entertainment, but it wasn't going anywhere. He reminded me too much of Mister. Maybe that's why I liked him so much because his antics felt familiar. They didn't feel good, but the familiarity was comfortable.

I was rotating my bench all around. Did I mention that Nani and I were back hanging out? We'd been hanging out ever since I put my clown suit back on in May. It was on and off, but it was more consistent now. He still had his live-in girlfriend, but he kept telling me he was trying to break it off with her. Honestly, I had learned at this point that some people look for help, not love. Back in May I truly felt bad for him being stuck in an unhappy relationship. But several months later, he was still in that same situation. He didn't want to get out, he was comfortable. He wasn't looking for love and he wasn't interested in taking me seriously, and I returned the favor. I knew he had nothing to offer me as a man but his company, so I took that. He would come over and hang out early in the morning or late at night. He never spent the night, though. I can only assume he and his girlfriend had a "just come home at night" agreement. I had completely gone to savage mode and told myself she wasn't my problem. I told him that when he came over, we didn't talk about her because it was MY time. Spoken like a true side piece. I was the weekend.

The less I pressed him, the harder he fell. It wasn't my problem, though. He and I both knew it wasn't going anywhere. One night we were hanging out and he asked, "I bet you're dating, huh?" I laughed and responded, "Well, yea." In disbelief, he said "I bet you're serious too." I stopped what I was doing to look at him to make things clear. "Why wouldn't I be? You have a whole girlfriend." He was hurt and disappointed. It didn't concern me. He was used to running over females, and that wasn't going to happen with me again. I was not going to sit at home and be a faithful side piece. I was still running the streets, and he needed to understand that.

Part of me could not understand how I had let myself get in this position, becoming the woman I despised; and the other part of me gave absolutely no care at all. I was a side piece, but not the typical side piece. He did try to have sex with me, but I wouldn't let him. Although we "messed around" he wasn't going to be able to claim these cookies. I couldn't fathom the thought of sleeping with him and then he goes home to a warm bed while I lie there confused in a cold bed. Maybe I wasn't as savage as I thought. I had a little common sense left. Not much, but a smidgen. I told him, "You're not going to come over here, break me off, then go home and leave me out in the cold. I'll be knocking at your door asking your girlfriend, is it my night?" He laughed and responded, "See, that's what I like about you." I knew then that he was crazy and that he wouldn't be getting any panty drawls.

Being lonely can take you to some dark places that only Jesus Himself can pull you out of. I was on a downward spiral. I could see myself headed down a path of destruction, but I couldn't stop myself.

One night in October, Chikae called me. Nothing out of the ordinary. We talked from time to time. He asked if my house was clean and told me to straighten up if it wasn't. He was like me—always traveling somewhere, but I had a hunch he was close to Louisiana. After exchanging conversation for a few minutes, he asked for my address and I knew then that he was close.

A few hours later, he showed up. I couldn't help thinking, "Why does this man get finer with time...why do men age so well?" Anyway, we headed to a local bar to get out of the house and catch up. He was telling me about the drama in his life and blamed me for turning him into a savage. We laughed as if it was a joke, but I knew it had some truth to it. He asked how Mister was doing. I told him I didn't know because we didn't talk anymore. I told him all I knew is that he was getting married in about a month. He was astonished. He knew how I felt about Mister and told me he just knew he and I were getting married. I must have not looked well because he kept asking me if I was ok after that. I assured him I was fine, and we didn't have to keep talking about it.

I truly hated that I had trouble expressing my feelings and resorted to, "I'm good, I'm fine, or I'm ok." The truth was I was not ok. I was acting out because I had suppressed all of my feelings about Mister and his new relationship. I felt like after all the drama he put me through he didn't deserve a good woman. He deserved to hurt like he hurt me, he deserved to suffer in the crazy dating world like I was. It wasn't fair. How could he marry her on a day we talked about getting married on and in a location where we discussed getting married? Not to mention, we'd just had a family vacation there. He was giving her everything he promised me, and that was a slap in the face. It hurt. It hurt more that he moved on and I felt stuck. I wanted him to be happy, just not that fast. Why couldn't I just get over him?

Chikae and I finished up our drinks and headed back

to my place to call it a night. I headed to my shower, and he asked if we could shower together. I know what you're thinking, and you're wrong. I told him no. One, I like my showers 200 plus degrees and two, it's my meditation time. There I was in the shower allowing the hot lava to melt the stress away and the curtain opened. There stands a naked chocolate man. I've always been a sucker for him, so I let him in. It was nothing sexual at all; we literally just showered together. It was extremely intimate. I finished up, got out, and moisturized my skin because it's a must, and we headed to bed.

I didn't like or let a lot of guys spend the night, but Chikae was an exception, of course. Cuddling was nice. It had been a while since I had true affection. We laid there silently for a few minutes and then he asked, "Can I eat it?" I knew this line all too well. It was the equivalent of "Just let me put the head in." I knew this place, it was familiar. 1 Corinthians 6:18 tells us to flee lust. We aren't strong enough to fight lust, so I was supposed to flee, right? I told him, "No." He asked again. I told him "no" again. I was doing good. I didn't need to flee. I was fighting this time—with my mouth anyway...but my heart and body had already said "Yes".

He implored and started touching me softly. There I was sliding my panties off, questioning how I got here, again. After the last encounter with Kola, I went to purchase condoms, so at least it was protected sex...until it wasn't. Somehow, halfway through, the condom went "missing". He pulled the condom off without me knowing. I'm not sure how many strokes had taken place unprotected, but I knew it was time to stop. He didn't seem concerned, but I was. I was in no place to get caught up in a sticky situation.

I couldn't believe that it happened again. Two partners in two weeks and both were unprotected. I was beating myself up considering the worst case scenarios. What if I was pregnant or caught something? I wouldn't even know whose baby it was or where I got the STD from. I was out of control. I called Sage in the morning having a minor panic attack asking if she thought I should go to the clinic. As a nurse, I knew nothing was going to show up that fast, but I was a wreck. How did I get to this place? Who was I? She helped me calm down and got me back to a place where I could think clearly.

After I pulled it together, I cooked breakfast for Chikae and I, and we hung out all day. We didn't bring up the night before. It felt like old times. We were laughing and clowning like we always had. We often questioned how things would be if we got back together, but he had kids now and I didn't date guys with kids for numerous reasons. I did miss him, though, but I knew it wasn't a good idea. He headed back that night to catch his early flight. There I was, alone, in my apartment thinking about who I'd become.

CHAPTER FIFTEEN

LOST

The next night Nani came over, as usual. He tried extra hard to get my panties, too. It had not even been 24 hours since I had sex and I wasn't about to let him get the panties just for him to go home and cuddle with his girlfriend. I had a few ounces of dignity left. I was ok with flirting and messing around, but we weren't about to go all the way. It made me feel a little better, I guess. He was crazy, too. He kept asking if I was dating and he didn't want me talking to other guys. For some reason, that night he asked when the last time I had sex was. Of course, I lied. I guess he didn't notice the hickey on my neck. He then proceeded to put one on the other side. He told me he had to go somewhere but would be back later to deliver...well, you know. I told him nah, I was good. He told me if I answered the phone, then it was a go and he was coming over.

I knew he was going to hit me up later. It was crazy how the tables turned from when we first met. I had let go of pressing him and he was eating out the palm of my hand. He did hit me up later, but I ignored it. I wasn't about to sleep with that man. I rolled over and went to sleep.

I didn't realize the closer it got to Mister's wedding day, the more I showed out. I couldn't be stopped. I didn't want to be a savage, but I was. I was doing guys how they'd been doing me. It was so bad, but I didn't even care. I was still talking to Mr. Incognito, Nani, Kola, and whoever else I met on the side. They were all in rotation. I stayed with Mister so long because I couldn't fathom being lonely, so I chose to be miserable. Now, I was just lonely and it had me making all kinds of questionable decisions.

HC2K16

Grambling's homecoming comes around. It was about to be epic because all the girls were going to be together. On Thursday, I spent all day getting ready. Nani came over that morning while I was straightening my hair and kept me company for a while. I told him that Talia and I were going to the comedy show, so he decided to go as well, but with his brother. I told him "Cool" and that I would see him there.

Talia and I headed to the show and cut up. We had a great time. Afterwards we headed out to eat. On the way to our seats, I was stopped by one of the hosts for the homecoming activities who happened to be a celebrity. We chatted for a little and he invited me to lunch the next day with him and his friends. I declined because he was married. I was

HERE LIES THE TRUTH

already entertaining a dude with a girlfriend, but I wasn't going to entertain a man with a wife. It was too familiar to me, and I wasn't that disrespectful. I headed to my seat and filled Talia in on what happened. She told me that Nani was sitting behind us. I checked my phone and there he was in my messages. I went over to speak. He was so jealous. He had watched the entire time when ol' boy was shooting his shot. I couldn't understand why he was jealous when he was the one in a relationship. Anywho, I thought it was perfect. He thought I had the juice and it humbled him, which he needed because he thought he was the man. We conversed for a few and then I went back to the table with Talia. We ate and drank until we were full and merry, then headed back to Monroe.

Friday came and it was on. All the girls were getting together. I packed a bag so I could spend the night at Brielle's house because I knew I was going to be intoxicated all weekend. Mr. Incognito was excited about homecoming too. He was hosting a party and it was all he talked about for months. He put so much effort into it. I didn't have a good feeling about the party because a lot of people weren't talking about it, but that wasn't my concern. The girls and I had other plans anyway. Nighttime fell, and we all met up at the Omega tailgate because Brielle and Dani are Deltas. We were out there skipping the line for chicken...just kidding! We were drinking, vibing, and conversing with old and new classmates and friends. I knew I had a little too much to drink when I saw a car roll by and asked if it was a Ferrari. It definitely was not a Ferrari and I knew that, but it slipped from my mouth. It was fine, though. I didn't drive, and I was off work for the entire weekend, so I kept drinking.

I hit up Mr. Incognito and asked how the party went. Why did I ever do that? He was hurt because the turnout wasn't what he expected. I didn't see the big deal. I mean, I was intoxicated. I figured I'd take him back to the house and cheer him up. I mean, I'd been "cheering" everyone else up. He thought I was still abstinent, and I let him think that. We went back to Brielle's house...and I'll leave it at that.

The next morning—or later that morning, I should say—his phone rang and woke us up. It was his homie calling asking where he was. He told him, "I'm at my girl's house right now, what's up?" I'm looking at him like, "Who's your girl?" I knew he was not talking about me. We hung out and spent time together, but I told him from jump street to not fall in love because I wasn't looking for that. Plus, he didn't take me seriously enough to date me, so there I was trying to figure out when I became his girl. Confused and still drunk, I watched him get dressed and leave. I walked him downstairs and tried to hurry him out before anyone saw me. After all, I was the "good girl". I went back upstairs, sat on the bed and thought about what I did. Again. I knew I was spiraling out of control, but I couldn't stop myself. I shrugged it off, as if my behaviors didn't bother me, showered, and got ready for another day of ratchet activities.

We all finally got dressed and were about to head out when Brielle got a call about her mom being in the hospital. Her family told her it was fine and there was no need to come up there. We stood in a circle, held hands, and I prayed for her mom's speedy recovery. We all touched in agreement, said amen, and went on to enjoy the day.

We got to the game, and it was packed. We're walking around single file, squeezing through people just to find a seat. I walked right past Nani and didn't even see him. I know he was feeling salty. Sage brought it to my attention as we settled on grass seats. He texted me and asked why I didn't speak, but I really didn't see him. It just added fuel to the fire from the day before. He was feeling like how he treats females, dismissed. It was funny how the tables had turned, from me sweating him to him checking for me. I can't lie, I kind of liked it.

After the game, I met up with my mom who happens to be a GSU alumna and a former band member. They were going to dinner with the other band members so she told me she would talk to me later. They left, so it was just Sage, my cousin, and me waiting on the others. We finally met up with the other girls and headed to scope out the parking lot. My cousin is an AKA and Brielle and Dani are Deltas. After we finished parking lot pimping, they wanted to check out their plots on campus, so we headed that way.

On the way, Mr. Incognito came up to me, hugged me, and grabbed my hand. I was mortified. I didn't want to be caught holding hands with him because we weren't dating. There were too many single men, and I was too single for anyone to be thinking otherwise. With bucked eyes and an anxiety attack on the horizon, I slowly pulled my hand away from his, cautiously scanning the crowd to make sure no one saw me. He had plenty of time to date and parade me around, but that's not what he wanted. He wasn't about to block my juice during homecoming. I told him I was going to hang with the girls and that I would hit him up later. Sage and I headed to the Delta plot first to meet Dani and Brielle. We chatted for a little while and decided to move around so they could enjoy their sorority sisters.

We saw an old friend who happened to be a member of a fraternity that shall remain unnamed. We headed that way to speak. He'd moved to a different state, and we hadn't seen him in a while. We caught up briefly trying to find the best move for the night. He told us about the alumni party. We told him we'd take it to the jury and decide. His friend came over to talk to him, and I started a conversation with him. He was so handsome, and he smelled good. I know what you're thinking...and you're exactly right. We exchanged conversation until the mosquitoes started to bite. He was such a gentleman, and I was already interested. We exchanged numbers and agreed to hang out that night at the alumni party.

We met back up with all the girls and headed back to the house to get ready for the night's shenanigans. After 17 hours of hair and makeup, we were all ready to go. Everybody was super cute—and super late as well—but we were prepared to turn heads. We headed to the bar to get drinks and headed to the dance floor to cut up. I saw Mr. Suave from earlier, but he paid me no never mind so I returned the same energy. As we were leaving, we managed to run into one another and spoke. He walked Talia and I to the car then asked what we were about to get into. Of course, it had to do with food. He told me to come by his hotel after we finished eating. I pondered it for a second and asked why he wanted me to come by. He said he just wanted to cuddle, and I told him he wasn't getting any cookies. He told me that was fine, he just wanted to hold me. A subconsciously broken soul, being held all night by this fine man sounded good to me.

Talia and I went back to Brielle's to grab some things and then she dropped me off at the hotel. I went to the room and knocked, ignoring the fact that I just met this guy and barely knew him. I kept thinking, "How did I get here?" I shushed my inner thoughts as he opened the door. We got in bed and talked for a little while until we fell asleep. We just cuddled, as he'd promised.

The sunrise woke me, along with the gentle touches of his hands. He kissed me in the mouth with my morning breath and all. I was thinking he must really like me. Who does that?! Kissing led to touching. He then begins to slide my panties down. Several thoughts cluttered my mind. One, I just had sex less than 24 hours ago. Two, I didn't even know this man, and three, something in my gut was saying, "DON'T DO IT SIS." I grabbed my panties and wiggled them back up and he got the picture. How did I get to this point? I had been living by—well, I was supposed to be living by—1 Corinthians 6:19-20, "What? know ye not that your body is the temple of the Holy Ghost which is in you, which ye have of God, and ye are not your own? For ye are bought with a price: therefore glorify God in your body, and in your spirit, which are God's.", I mean for crying out loud, it was the background on my phone. "Lord, help me please." We said our goodbyes and I proceeded to leave the room. On my way out, I noticed an open box of condoms on top of his bag. I shook my head and chuckled to myself. Thank goodness I listened to my gut. I got downstairs to wait for Talia to arrive. I sat there ashamed as I saw all the frat guys checking out of the hotel.

I felt disgusted. Not the type you could wash off in the shower. Being a savage didn't fix my broken heart. I just kept digging the hole deeper and deeper. I was in over my head and couldn't stop if I wanted to. The closer it got to Mister's wedding, the worse I behaved. Instead of confronting my feelings about our relationship and breakup, I kept suppressing. I pushed that beach ball underwater and it kept popping up in different areas of my life. It was destructive. Why wouldn't I just face the truth, the facts? Why couldn't I let go to save myself? My identity was wrapped up in being hurt and angry, but I was suppressing it. If I were to let go of the pain, what would I have? After all this time he still had control over me, and I hated it.

By this time, I was awfully consistent with making bad decisions. Have you ever felt so far gone that you don't even try to do better? I'd lost faith in myself that I could do better, so I was like, "What the heck?"

Kola was into fitness, so after I got some disappointing fake news from a local trainer, I turned to him. The trainer told me I had 42 percent body fat. Now friends, I worked out 4–5 days a week. I stood 5'1 130 pounds. 32–28–38. There was nothing obese about me. Ignorant to the body fat scale, I had to turn to someone I trusted, and that was Kola.

I called him to tell him what happened and to see if he could manually check my body fat. He assured me that he could and told me to come by. We spoke a little about fitness. He reassured me that I was not 42 percent body fat and showed me what that body type would look like. I felt 100 times better after speaking with him. He told me he'd left his equipment at the gym and would measure me next time he saw me. We started clowning and reminiscing, then one thing led to another. I know what you're thinking. No, I did not sleep with him again...not right then. I did make an appointment for later that night, though. I had made dinner plans with Brielle, Ircy, and Sage, and I was already running late. Remember, I told you God always gives you a way out, you just have to take it. Well, this was my way out.

I met with the girls for Mexican—and by Mexican, I mean margaritas, chips, and salsa. Just kidding. Not really. We enjoyed dinner and got caught up with each other's lives. Brielle and I decided to go to a party for her friend's birthday that night. I told her I had to make a pitstop, then I would be back to get ready. I gave her my house key and headed back to Kola's house. Had I gone home to get ready for the party, I wouldn't have been in this situation. God had already provided a way out, but I was too far gone in my downward spiral to listen. I arrived and told him, "Let's get to it because I have plans with my girlfriend and don't have time to spare." There we were ripping each other's clothes off, getting down to it. But there was a problem. There wasn't much business going on, if you know what I mean. We had some trouble getting the engine to turn over. After several minutes passed, I asked, was it me? He assured me that it wasn't me, but that didn't make me feel any better. Disappointed, I gathered my things and headed toward the door. We exchanged good-byes and I left.

I rushed home because I had kept Brielle waiting. On the drive home, I did some reflecting and decided that I needed to block his number. I loved him and he was everything I wanted in a man. Sadly, he didn't feel the same about me. I'd reduced myself to play whatever part I could in his life, and that was disappointing. I just wanted to be around him. It didn't matter the cost. Doubly disappointed, I sulked. I got home, told Brielle about my less than satisfying experience, and we laughed. But I laughed to hold back the tears. Why I couldn't stop myself from this self-destructing behavior wasn't funny. I found myself in the shower trying to wash myself clean only to find that the top layer of dirt was the only dirt that washed down the drain. I knew I needed to do better, but how? I was too far gone, ignoring God's warning signs, and we all know that before destruction comes warnings.

We headed to the club to turn up with her friend. I headed straight to the bar to forget the events that had taken place earlier that night. While at the bar, a guy from the gym that I know started buying Brielle and I shots. Well, we didn't want to be rude, so we took the shots. I drank all night trying to numb the pain of rejection, regret, and disappointment. Before the end of the night, she slipped him my number. He was very handsome so, of course, I didn't mind. It was just my luck, though. I realized through talking to him that he was thug life. Like, "been to jail, feds watching, slangin'" thug life. I had a little self-respect left and severed that relationship fast. I couldn't be caught up in that life. I had enough going on, and I wasn't trying to be a ride-or-die chick.

The following Tuesday, I pulled up to the gym and received a phone call. It was about Brielle's mom. She'd been in and out of the hospital for the past two weeks. The last report I'd received was that she was doing great and was about to be discharged. The phone call was informing me that there was a rumor going around that she passed away. I got irritated because I knew it was a lie. I couldn't understand why people in that little town would make up such a horrid rumor because you're not supposed to speak death on people. I got off the phone so that I could call Brielle to make sure the plan was still to discharge Mama that day and to see how she was doing. The phone rang...and rang. No answer. I called a couple of times. When she didn't answer, I started to worry. I called Dani and she gave me some hard news to swallow. I sat in the car and screamed as I banged on my steering wheel trying to make sense of what I'd just heard. I was angry and I was in disbelief. Most importantly, I hated this for my friend because last year had been extremely rough on her.

I did about 100 MPH trying to get to the hospital. I was praying and wiping tears the entire way as I rode in silence. When I arrived, I saw her brother outside, I hugged him and said, "I don't know what to say." That was unusual because I always had something to say. I rushed inside the hospital and hugged Dani. A few tears escaped my eyes, but I caught them quickly because I had to be strong for my friend.

People were in and out of the room crying and praying. I walked into the room with Dani and looked at Mama as she lay there peacefully. She looked as if she was sleeping. I hugged Brielle and wept quietly. I knew it hurt, and there was nothing I could do to fix it. I just wanted to fix it for her. Since I couldn't do that, I just wanted to be in this moment and share my love with her as she hurt. I wanted her to know that I was there and that she could lean on me.

I remember the hallway being stale. There were innumerable emotions. Mama was a well of knowledge and wisdom. A friend and a shoulder to lean on, she always knew exactly what to say when you needed it. She was a light. I couldn't help but be angry with myself because Brielle was telling me all the things the hospital did. I kept thinking thoughts like, "That's not how it should be done, that's not right, that's absurd!" I kept thinking if I had just gone up there to check on her then she would still be here. Medical professionals are more cautious when they know there are other medical professionals checking in on their loved ones. But Brielle told me her mom didn't want many visitors and I respected that. I couldn't help but feel guilty, though. I prayed for God to heal her and we touched in agreement. Did God not hear my prayer? Was He turning his ear from me because of my behavior? I couldn't help but think maybe I should have let someone else pray. It wasn't my place to feel sorry for myself at this time. It was about my friend and her family, so I put my feelings aside to focus on what was important.

As if this wasn't enough already, I look up and see Mister's mom (whom I absolutely love) walk through the door. We hugged and then I was reminded of the upcoming wedding. Like I didn't have enough to process already, there I stood making light of the wedding saying, "Oh yea that is coming up, you know he didn't invite me?" We both laughed and reminisced a second. She told me I was always welcome to come by, but I declined out of respect for him and his new relationship. There I was, again, putting his feelings before mine. She was like a mother to me. It hurt to have to sever our relationship.

I called in to work and stayed with Brielle that night. I didn't want her to be alone. She had a long journey ahead of her. I made sure she was ok the next day and headed to work. I was on a travel assignment 3.5 hours away from home, so I had a lot of time to think, cry, and pray.

All I wanted was a shoulder to cry on, a man's arms to hold me and contain the complete wreck I'd become, but all I had was unreliable part-time lovers. I wanted Nani to be there for me so badly, but he couldn't. He had a place at home, and I wasn't a part of that. That never bothered me before. I knew how to play my part and was good at it. This time was different; I was broken. I was angry that he couldn't, or wouldn't, be there and I realized we had nothing but a few stolen good times. It opened my eyes to the statement he always made: "I wish I could give you more." It was then that it hit me. I realized we were going around in circles, and I was ready to get off the merry-go-round.

I told myself I deserved more. I deserved better. Not that I believed that, but I figured if I kept telling myself those words, one day I would believe them. I was done. I was hurting and our situation wasn't making it any better. After this late epiphany, I blocked his number. Not only did I block his number, I also deleted our entire text thread. I was done, done. Two guys down one more to go. I was watching my starting five disappear and it was extremely uncomfortable; but when you're ready for change, you have to change.

I was exhausted, physically, emotionally, spiritually, and mentally. I was done being a savage because instead of fixing my heart, it broke my heart even more. I wasn't the person I had been pretending to be. Running wild, living life without care and apathetic to the consequences of my detrimental actions. I was ready to face my truth. I knew it was going to be tough, but when you're tired, I mean really tired, you will do what it takes to change.

CHAPTER SIXTEEN

FOUND

I found myself staring at the stitching in the car-pet...damp tissue clinched in my hand. I was taking turns be-tween wiping my snotty nose and wiping tears that escaped my eyes as I kept saying, "I'm sorry." I felt her eyes reading me. I mumbled, "I said I wasn't going to cry, but I'm so tired of being strong, tired of pretending to be a savage, tired of faking it." She told me, "It's ok to cry." Everything was so wrong in my life, and I hated it. I was honest and raw with her, and I didn't feel judged. It was the first time I accepted that I could not do it on my own and I needed help. I knew I needed Jesus and a counselor, and I was ok with that. I felt bricks being lifted as I poured out my anger and pain to her.

She gave me homework assignments, like confronting my feelings and being honest with people about my feelings.

It was hard and uncomfortable. I often suppressed my feelings and didn't let people know how they'd hurt me. She
encouraged me to confront them, and I did. I started working
the program and I saw a change in myself. I was happier. I
was calm. I was peaceful.

Not even two weeks after I started counseling, I met
someone new: Marco. Yeah, yeah, "another one", a new
one—as if I needed to be talking to anyone. I was an emotional wreck, but he was sweet. He was consistent and considerate. He texted back, called on the phone, wasn't in a relationship, and didn't have any kids. He wasn't trying to play
games, and that made him stand out to me. I felt like I could
be myself. I didn't have to play games to keep his attention.
He had a good head on his shoulders and seemed to be a
good catch. I was moving to California in less than 3 months,
and I wasn't trying to date or get attached to anyone. So, I
didn't see how this could hurt.

We talked and went on dates up until I left for California in January. I knew things would fizzle out and I was ok
with that, even though I really liked him. I just wanted to enjoy traveling, being single, and being free. I had turned over
a new leaf and things were looking up for me. 2016 was a
terrible year and I professed that 2017 would be a better
year. I claimed peace, happiness, and restoration.

Just as I was sure things were going to fizzle out, I was
completely wrong. Marco and I grew even closer. They say
absence makes the heart grow fonder. He kept asking me to
be his girlfriend, but he wasn't where I needed him to be
spiritually, and that was a red flag...well, stop sign. I wasn't
where I needed to be spiritually, so I couldn't entertain

someone who didn't want to understand what I believed. Sounds good in theory, right? But I already loved him; how was I supposed to let go? Being unequally yoked was a non-negotiable for me, but I negotiated. I figured he could learn to love God the way I did, or maybe I could love him into being saved.

I started fasting from alcohol. I said I would start drinking again after he got saved. I thought I could "fast" him into being saved. I fasted and I prayed for God to show me whether or not I needed to proceed into a relationship with him. That was something I did not even need to pray about. I was blinded because he was so nice to me and considerate. He wasn't like any other guy I had met before. After going through hell with men for the last 5 years, he was a breath of fresh air. I wasn't willing to give that up without a fight.

So, we started dating and things were great. We hardly ever argued, we communicated well, and were considerate of one another. We spent time together when we could and traveled quite a bit. He was open to trying new things and I appreciated that. Things were going well and heading for an engagement. I mean, he did ask me to go get sized for rings. If I jumped the gun and that means something else, let me know.

I knew I loved him and cared for him, but if we're being honest, I knew I would never agree to becoming his wife unless we were equally yoked. Not only spiritually, but mentally as well. I wanted it so badly, I could see the finish line. In addition to thinking I could "fast" him into being who I wanted him to be, I thought if I just loved him hard enough, he would change.

It wasn't long before our relationship became strained. I knew after a few months that it wasn't going to work, but I thought maybe things would get better. God told me to leave, but I ignored his instruction. I was waiting for a "bigger sign", just to be sure. Sure enough, the last couple of months things got bad. I had become quite unhappy and decided to break it off with him the next time I saw him.

CHAPTER SEVENTEEN
MORE LIFE

Sage came to town to spend some time with me, and I really needed her because I needed her to talk me through my emotions. I needed her to validate that I wasn't crazy and that things were bad between Marco and me. She never validates, but helps me realize what I already know and helps me sort my emotions. We did our session then got ready for the weekend of shenanigans we had planned. We cut up the entire weekend. By the time Sunday came, we were exhausted.

We slept in and decided to go get lunch when we woke up. While at lunch, I told her I hadn't been feeling my best and that I had been so exhausted lately. I told her I had a lot on my plate and was just trying to figure out my next move. She assured me it was just stress. I told her, "I hope so because I'm late." I know stress can make you late, but I was never late. We joked around toying with the idea of me having a baby, it was humorous. It wasn't going to happen to me. I mean, if it was going to happen, it would have already happened by now. I always professed, "I'll never have a baby out of wedlock." We agreed to go get a pregnancy test after we finished eating just to calm my nerves.

We headed to the store to get the tests. I purchased three just in case I messed it up. When we got home, I rushed to the bathroom because I'd been holding it. I ripped open the pack and read the instructions as I did the potty dance. I threw the box across the counter and began the test. The results came so fast. I hollered to Sage laughing, "GIRL, TWO LINES MEAN NEGATIVE RIGHT?!?" She ran to the bathroom. She grabbed the box and stared at it. Without looking at me, she solemnly said, "Ummmm...no, it says two lines means positive."